Schools of the Nine Demon Gods

KUKISHIN RYU
BOJUTSU KIHON

BY KOBA KOSHIRO
TRANSLATED BY ERIC SHAHAN

Translator's Note:

This is a translation and reproduction of the first section of the martial arts instruction manual:

School of the Nine Demon Gods: Martial Arts Collection
All-Japan Self-Defense
Volume One: Bojutsu
By Koba Koshiro
Supervised by Viscount Kuki Takaharu
Published by the Society for Promoting the Shinto
Religion With the Emperor as its Divine Head
Published in 1936

This volume will cover the origins of the School of the Nine Demon Gods, basic stances, basic attacks and training sequences. The second volume will cover Hanbo, Half-Staff techniques and the third volume will cover Rokushakubo, Six Foot Staff Techniques.

Each page will be reproduced on the left hand side with the English translation on the right hand side. For some techniques, the explanation and photographs are not on the same page, therefore the photographs will be reproduced again for clarity.

Kukishin Ryu Martial Arts Collection

All Japan Self-Defense
Volume One: Bojutsu
By Koba Koshiro
1936

Seigo Hyo
Corrections After Publication

正誤表

頁	行	誤字	正
自序一	七	實踐	實戰
二〇	二	の懸け鑿	四の懸け撃
五六	第五十五圖	左横へを打ちたる處	左胴を打ちたる處
同	一	左霞	右霞
七	九	左技―右技	右技
七五	一	右段	左霞
九	四	左足	右足
一〇	一〇	右足	左足
二一	三	右手	左手
二二	十一	右足	右手
一四	六	左足を一歩前に跨み出して横	元の位置につきて棒を
二五	四	左足を退き棒を	棒を引き
一四	一	左足	右足
一四	九	右足を前	右足を右前隅
一六	四	右足	左足
一七	一〇	横へて殘心を示す	棒へる
一九八	一	如くに面を打つ	如くに面を打つ
同	六	次で右膊	次で右足を一歩踏み出すと共に右膊
二三五	一	左脛	左脛

Seigo Hyo
Corrections After Publication

This is a chart added after printing noting some errors in the text. They mostly consist of mistakenly writing right 右 instead of left 左, or vice versa, however there are a couple of minor corrections to how Kata are done. These corrections will all be included in the translation.

皇道宣揚會總裁從三位子爵　九鬼隆治校閱
皇道宣揚會尚武局長　教範　木葉幸四郎著

九鬼神流
武術叢書

大日本護身術

第一編
棒術

發行所

皇道宣揚會尚武局支部道場

Kukishin Ryu Bujutsu Sosho
School of the Nine Demon Gods Martial Arts Collection
Dainihon Goshin Jutsu
All Japan Self-Defense
Dai Ippen Bojutsu
Volume One: Staff Fighting
By Koba Koshiro
Supervised by Viscount Kuki Takaharu

Published by *Kodo Senyo* "Society for Promoting the Shinto Religion With the Emperor as its Divine Head."[1]

---

[1] This society was founded in 1934 for the purpose of promoting the Shinto religion.

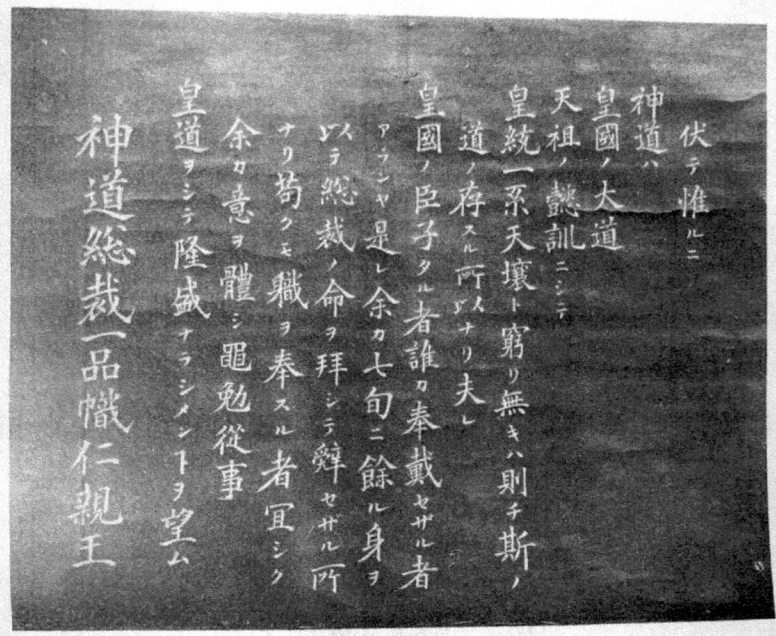

皇道之令旨

伏テ惟ルニ

神道ハ

皇国ノ大道

天祖ノ懿訓ニシテ

皇統一系天壌ト窮リ無キハ則チ斯ノ

道ノ存スル所以ナリ夫レ

皇国ノ臣子タル者誰力奉戴セザル者

アランヤ是レ余力七句ニ餘ル身ヲ

以テ総裁ノ命ヲ拝シテ辭セザル所

ナリ苟クモ職ヲ奉スル者宜シク

余力意ヲ體シ黽勉從事

皇道ヲシテ隆盛ナラシタン「ヲ臨ム

神道総裁一品幟仁親王

A decree announcing the founding of the Society for Promoting the Shinto Religion With the Emperor as its Divine Head.

Reflecting Carefully
Shinto is
The Great Way of this imperial land
The sublime teachings of the founder of the Kingdom of Heaven
The Imperial Lineage is as limitless as heaven and earth.
This is why the teachings of Shinto exist.
Who else other than the Emperor would loyal vassals choose to lead?

With these seven lines I accept the duty to become the director.
I will dedicate myself to follow my duty with diligence and devotion with every fiber of my being.
So that the Way of the Emperor be allowed to flourish.

Written by His Imperial Highness Prince Arisugawa Takahito
Director of the Department of Shinto Affair[2]

---

[2] Prince Arisugawa Takahito 有栖川宮幟仁親王(1813~1886) was the eighth head of one of the branches of the Imperial Family of Japan, which were eligible to succeed in the event that the main line should die out. He was also the first director of the Department of Shinto Affairs, and was influential in the development of State Shinto. State Shinto began in the Meiji Era and encouraged the practice of Shinto and Japanese folk religion that emphasized the Emperor as a divine being.

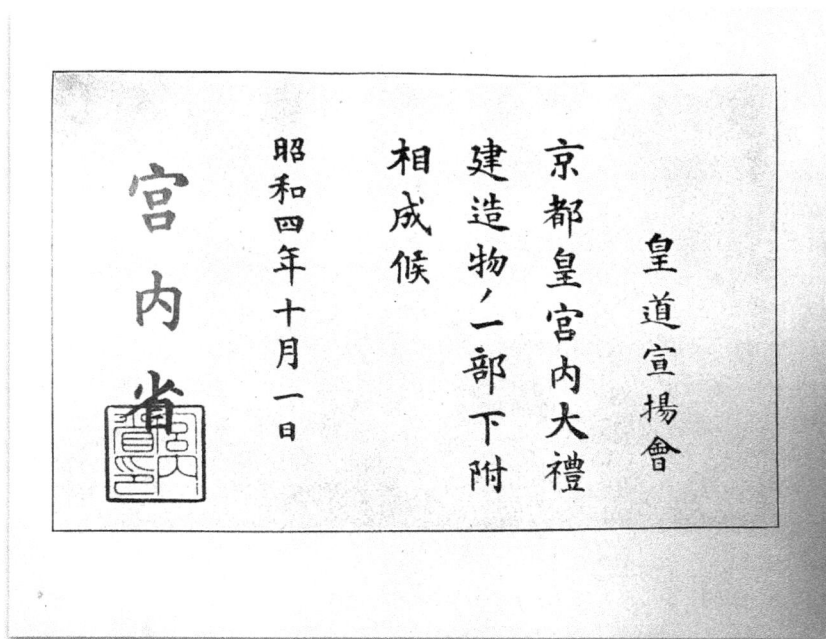

Document from the Ministry of the Imperial Household granting the Society for Promoting the Shinto Religion With the Emperor as its Divine Head a building in Kyoto.
September 1st Showa 4 (1929)

The Society for Promoting the Shinto Religion With the Emperor as its Divine Head donated a building to go over the sacred well that was used for the enthronement ceremony of His Majesty the Emperor. The Society also donated one set of implements necessary to use the sacred well.

高御位山神宮遥拝所

A Jinguyohaijo Shrine atop Mount Takamikura in Hyogo Prefecture. Jinguyohaijo Shrines are dedicated to honoring the Shinto gods and the head of the religion on earth, the Emperor of Japan. The goal was to veneration the myths found in the earliest texts such as Chronicles of Japan and by suppressing Buddhism and folk beliefs

Painting of Kuki Yoshitaka 九鬼嘉隆 (1542 ~ 1600)

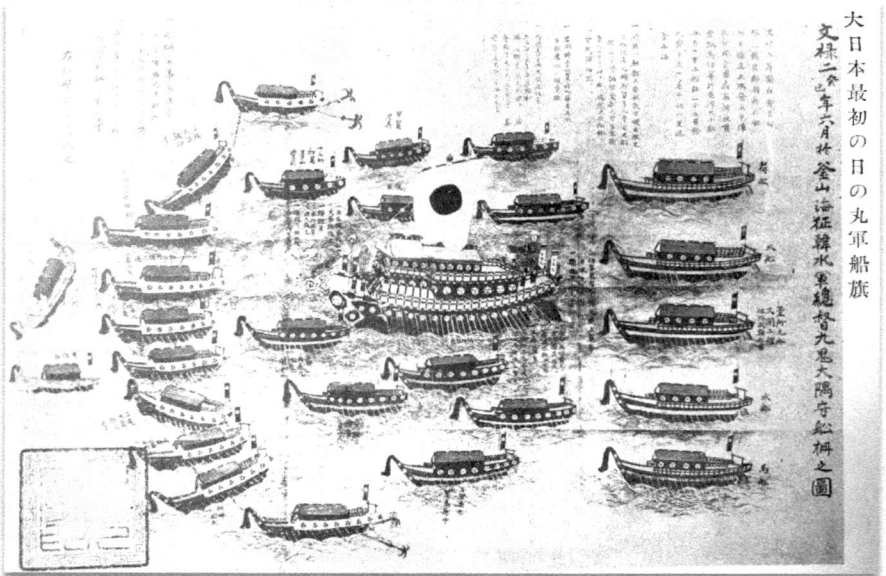

Illustration of the 1593 fleet led by Kuki Yoshitaka which was the
first to fly the Hinomaru, the flag that is today's national flag.

Honorable Advisors to
The Society for Promoting the Shinto Religion With the
Emperor as its Divine Head

問 顧 譽 名 會 揚 宣 道 皇

公爵 近衛文麿閣下

His Excellency Duke Konoe Fumimaro

侯爵 小松輝久閣下

His Excellency
Marquis Teruhisa Komatsu

公爵 一條實孝閣下

His Excellency
Duke Ichijo Sanetaka

Honorable Supporters of
The Society for Promoting the Shinto Religion With the Emperor as its Divine Head

皇道宣揚會名譽協賛員

伯爵 清浦圭吾閣下

His Excellency Count Kiyoura Keigo

子爵 小笠原長生閣下

His Excellency Viscount
Ogasawara Naganari

男爵 荒木貞夫閣下

His Excellency
Baron Araki Sadao

下閣治隆鬼九 爵子 裁總

General Director Viscount Kuki Takaharu

郎五辰田島 頭會

President Shimada
Tatsugoro

下閣清重內岡 爵男 裁總副

Assistant Director His Excellency
Baron Okauchi Shigetoshi

教範 松原嘉平
Instructor Matsubara Kahei

教範 木葉幸四郎
Instructor Koba Koshiro

教監 鹽崎勝夫
Instructing Supervisor
Shiozaki Katsuo

教範 小寺武司
Instructor Kodera Takeshi

The Naobu Kyoku Dojo of the Society for Promoting the Shinto Religion With the Emperor as its Divine Head

In front of the Honcho, Main Dojo, of the Naobu Kyoku Dojo of the Society for Promoting the Shinto Religion With the Emperor as its Divine Head

Photograph of How Training is Conducted

自序

九鬼神流棒術は本會頭神祇伯大中臣熊野別當九鬼家祖傳にして日本國粹武藝なり。

後醍醐天皇の御宇熊野別當藥師丸藏人公南朝に奉仕して逆臣尊氏を調伏したる當時棒を以て逆賊を撃退せしめ大功を奏したるに始まる。

其後弓術馬術槍術劍術柔術薙刀術等と共に並行して工夫研究し九鬼神流武術は彌々完成し盛んに練磨せられ逐時諸勇士偉人等實踐に於て偉勳を顯したる事蹟は記録に依り既に明かにして普く研究せられたる九鬼神流武術も明治維新以來時代の變遷と共に西洋思想輸

一

Introduction

The Kukishin Ryu Bojutsu being taught by the head of this organization is transmitted through the Kuki family and has become the premier martial art in Japan. The Kuki family held many titles. They were the Singihaku, Head of the Department of Worship, the O-Nakaomi, in charge of conducting religious ceremonies, and were designated the Kumano Betto, in charge of administering the Three Kumano Head Shrines.[3]

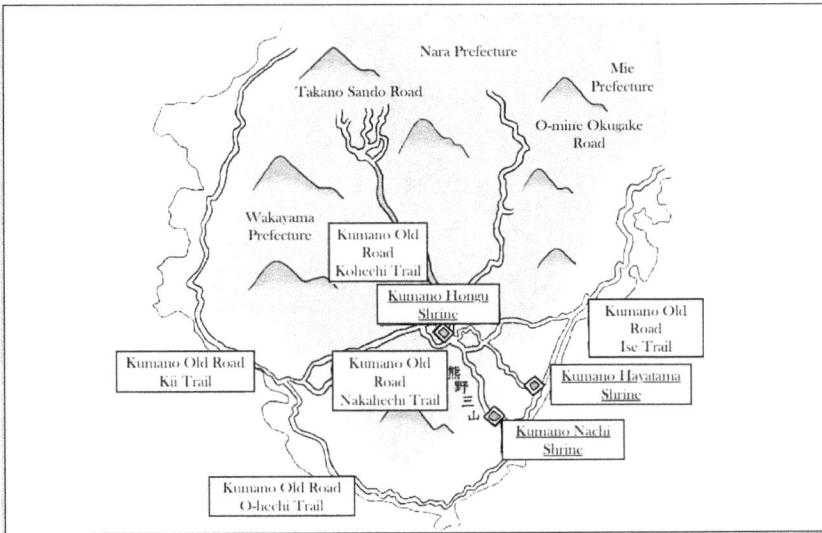

---

[3] *O-Nakaomi* is a hereditary position that is in charge of rites and ceremonies related to gods and ancestors.

Kumano Betto is a hereditary position supervising the Kumano Sanzan, Three Kumano Head Shrines. There are more than 3,000 Kumano shrines in Japan each of which enshrines the three Kumano mountains: Hongu, Hayatama and Nachi.

The temples are all connected as each has received its Kami from another Kumano shrine through a process of propagation known as *Bunrei* 分霊 "dividing the spirit." The Kumano shrines are generally between 12~25 miles apart and are connected to each other by a pilgrimage route known as the Kumano Old Road.

Translator's Note:

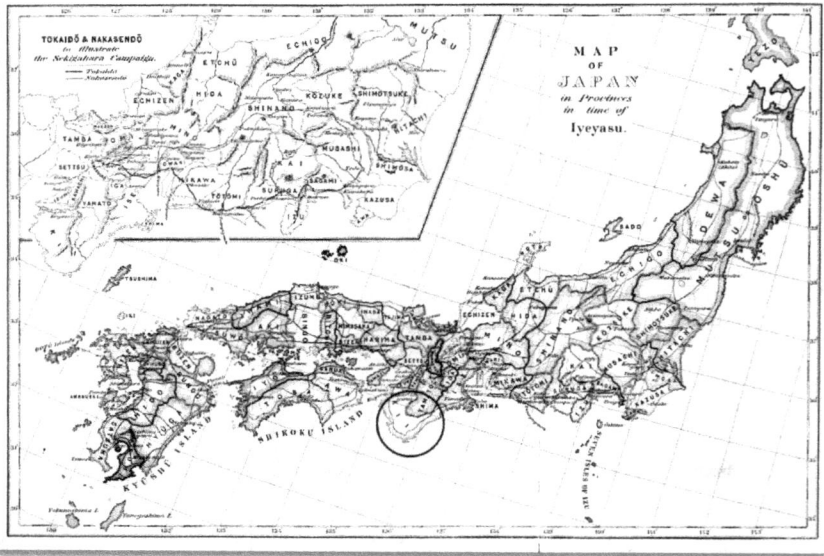

Location of the Three Kumano Head Shrines. In the 1600s this area was known as Kii Domain which is present day Wakayama Prefecture.

During the reign of Emperor Daigo, the man supervising the Three Kumano Shrines, Lord Yakushi Maruku-rando subdued a revolt by Ashikaga Takauji. In that battle he used a Bo in order to drive off the usurpers, achieving a great victory, which was the beginning of his success.

Following this he began to add other martial arts to his school including Kyujutsu (archery,) Bajutsu (equestrian,) Sojutsu (spear fighting,) Kenjutsu (sword fighting,) Jujutsu (unarmed fighting,) Naginata Jutsu (halberd) and others. Maruku-rando then worked to add his own developments to each of these arts and eventually, after rigorous training, completed the formation of Kukishin Ryu Bujutsu, The Nine Demon Gods School of Martial Arts. Over the years many brave warriors and great men have demonstrated the utility of these techniques to great acclaim their actions are a matter of record.

However, the upheaval and changes that took place with the advent of the Meiji Restoration even those studying Kukishin School martial arts were affected. Further, the importation of Western thought had the unfortunate effect of causing the Japanese people to forget Budo Seishin, marital arts spirit, which is the very essence of Japan. This resulted in even the art of Bojutsu fading from the consciousness of the people.

自序　二

入せられ國粹武道精神は惜哉閑却して殊に棒術の如きは衰頽し將に

世人の記憶を脱せんとするに至る。

明治拾參年講道館柔道同二十八年武德會武術等起りて體育的武道

漸く唱導せらるゝに及び、久しく顧みられざりし九鬼神流武術も各地

に支部道場を設けて皇道宣揚と武道精神の普及に務めし結果共鳴す

る士は之れを修めんと年々續出し來るを見る時邦家の爲め欣幸とす

る所なり。

然るに斯界諸賢の士は斯道研究の書を余に求むるの聲高し茲に於

て不肯淺學菲才を以て皇道宣揚に力を致し國家の寄託に添はんもの

と從來實施指導せし儘を記述し大方の期待に應へん覺悟とす、惜むら

In the 13th year of Meiji (1880) the Kodokan was founded and in the 28th year (1895) the Butokukai Bujutsu society was founded meaning that after a long hiatus there was a return to advocating physical training through martial arts.

Thus, thanks to these developments, the long neglected Kukishin School of Martial Arts is now opening branch Dojos in every area, which are working to promote both the Society for Promoting the Shinto Religion With the Emperor as its Divine Head and Budo Seishin, Martial Arts Mentality. The result being that the number of gentleman-warriors who these two topics resonate with are increasing year after year. This is a joyous thing for our country.

Recently many of these gentleman-warriors have asked for me to write a book on how training should be done in this school of martial arts. Therefore, despite the fact that I have only a superficial understanding of the material and am of only limited ability, I was able to write this book. Due to the support of the society during this endeavor I feel I will be able to meet the public's expectations.

In that regard, I am resolved to use this book to describe the same training method that was taught in the past. I regret to say that, for a time, I was so busy with the affairs of the association that I was not able to find the time to complete this project.

くは會務に忙殺せられ其暇を得ざりしと尚ほ唯微力の及はざらんことを恐る幸ひ此の機會に於て同志先賢の努力と援助を仰がれんことを乞ふ。

昭和十一年十一月十日

著者識

Now that I have completed this book, I am afraid that my efforts are inadequate for this great duty. I was only able to complete it due to the the efforts of my comrades and senior members of the Society.

By the Author
November 10th of Showa 11 (1936)

凡例

一、本書は大中臣熊野別當九鬼家祖傳たる九鬼神流武術中の棒術九字九通九十九本より其の粹を拔き取捨折衷し以て皇道宣揚會武術として復棒術實地活用的正技として悉く之れを收めたるを以て斯道修業者に採りて萬遺漏なきを期す。

一、本書は明治維新以來殆んど廢絕したる九鬼神流棒術の秘法を公開し國民一般に普及奬勵して士氣の涵養振作其の實踐を期せんがために著述せるものなり。

一、本書は其の內容を第五章に頒ち難解に寫眞を揷入し以て說明を

凡例

Honrei
Introductory Remarks

- This book contains the Bojutsu section of the Kukishin School of martial arts handed down in the Kuki family. This family served as both the O-Nakaomi and Kumano Betto. This book has selected the techniques that best represent the essence of this school from the *Kuji Kutsu Kyujukyu*, Ninety-nine Techniques Infused With the Power of the Nine Seals,[4] and eliminated the rest. The techniques selected form part of the official martial arts techniques of the Society for Promoting the Shinto Religion With the Emperor as its Divine Head and will serve to assist in developing the mental health and physical development of the Japanese people. Further, Bojutsu is a practical method that can be applied in real situations. This complete system covers every aspect of Bojutsu and practitioners of this art can be absolutely assured that there are no omissions.

- This book consists of the Hiho, secret teachings, of Kukishin Ryu Bojutsu that were all but lost following the Meiji Restoration. These methods are now being released to the general public and it is my hope that what is written here will succeed in encouraging fighting spirit and cultivating practical skills.

- This book has been divided into five chapters and, due to the difficulty of the material, photographs have been included along with the explanations in order to make remembering the lessons easier.

---

[4] This is referring to Kuji 九字 the Nine Seals. Originally this was a charm to banish evil when entering a mountain range, however when it was adopted by Mikkyo and Shugendo practitioners the spell became away to guard the body. A set of nine hand gestures are done while chanting Rin 臨, Pyo 兵, Toh 闘, Sha 者, Kai 皆, Jin 陣, Retsu 列, Zai 在, Zen 前 before cutting a series of lines with your finger. The lines cut with the fingers form a boundary against evil spirits.

凡例

加へて了解記憶に易からしむ。

一、本書は卷頭に明治天皇詔勅、神道總裁有栖川宮幟仁親王令旨、宮內省御下賜御神井戸上屋、神宮遙拜所、國寶九鬼大隅守嘉隆公肖像、日本最初の日の丸軍船旗、小德冠者、九鬼藥師丸隆眞公傳授兵法の卷の一部、皇道宣揚會、名譽顧問、名譽協贊員、皇道宣揚會高御位山本廳道場、道場內部、棒術練習實況等の口繪寫眞を插入し、本文には基本八法九字の形、半棒、六尺棒等約六十六本を說明し、卷尾には皇道宣揚會趣旨綱領、皇道宣揚會伺武局道場規則等を記載したり。

一、本書は武道に心得あるものは勿論老若男女の別なく全く棒術の素養なきものも之れを會得し易くして其の妙技神術を最も平易に

二

- The first section of this book included the following material: A decree announcing the founding of the Society for Promoting the Shinto Religion With the Emperor as its Divine Head, a document from the Ministry of the Imperial Household granting the Society a building in Kyoto, a photograph of the building donated by the Society to go over the sacred well that was used for the enthronement ceremony of His Majesty Emperor Hirohito. A photograph of a Jinguyohaijo Shrine atop Mount Takamikura in Hyogo Prefecture. A section of the Martial Arts Sword Scroll transmitted to Lord Kuki Yakjushi Marurikushin by Shotoku Kanja,[5] a painting of Kuki Yoshitaka, a painting of the fleet led by Kuki Yoshitaka that was the first to fly the Hinomaru, the flag that is today's national flag. It also introduces the members of the Honorable Advisors and Honorable Supporters of The Society, as well as photographs both inside and outside the Naobu Kyoku Dojo in addition to a photograph of how training is conducted.

  The text contains explanations of how to do the Kihon Happo Kuji no Kata, Hanbo and Rokushakubo.[6] Over sixty-six Kata in total. At the end of the book will be an overview of the Society for Promoting the Shinto Religion With the Emperor as its Divine Head as well as the rules and regulations for the Society's Bukyoku martial arts Dojo.

- The lessons on martial arts contained in this volume can be used by anyone, man, woman, old or young. Even a complete novice can use this knowledge to easily develop their skill in Bojutsu. To make this marvelous martial arts system accessible to everyone, it be explained using plain language. Learners will be guided from having only a cursory knowledge to developing a deep grasp of the techniques. This method is ideal for learning on your own and will allow you easily grasp the essence.

---

[5] This picture was not included in the book though there do not appear to be any missing pages.

[6] Kihon Happo Kuji no Kata – Eight Fundamental Method Transfused with Kuji.

Hanbo – Half-staff. Rokushakubo – Six Shaku Long Wooden Staff.

凡例

一、通俗的に説明せるを以て、淺きより深きに不識々々導き獨習に便なる旨意に出でたるものなり。

一、本書中八法九字の形は相手なくとも單獨にて練習し得るを以て一般家庭の體育運動として又學校其他團體等に武術的體育法として最も適當するものなり。

一、本書を編纂するに本會頭總裁九鬼神流武術宗家從三位子爵九鬼隆治閣下の校閲を得たり茲に謹んで感謝す。

一、本書は著者の淺學菲才を以て專ら斯道の公開普及に努めたれば用語の不正説明の不徹底等の點尠しとせず乞ふ諸賢の批判を相俟つて正誤改粹せられんことを。

- The Happo Kuji no Kata, Eight Methods Infused with the Power of the Nine Seals, described in this volume can be trained easily without a partner and it can serve as a method of physical fitness for your household. Further, when compared to the physical education done in schools or in other martial arts organizations, it is the most effective martial arts exercise system.

- The author would like to thank receiver of Junior Third Rank and Soke of Kukishin Ryu Bujutsu General Director Viscount Kuki Takaharu for checking and approving this manuscript.

- The author is a man of meagre learning and even less ability, however he has dedicated himself to this path and released a book to promote this art. He begs your forgiveness for any unclear explanations or any errors in the text. Any errors brought to his attention will be corrected.

九鬼神流
武術叢書 大日本護身術
第一編 棒術 目次

目次

一

Kukishin Ryu Bujutsu Series
All Japan Self-Defense Techniques
Book One : Bojutsu

Chapter One

Kukishin Ryu Bojutsu no Kigen
The Origin of the Staff Techniques of the School of the Nine Demon Gods

Chapter Two

Reigi, Saho, Maai
Regarding Bowing, Manners and Distance

Chapter Three

Part One
Shisei, Kamae – Posture and Stance

1. *Hira Ichimonji no Kamae* – Open Front Stance
2. *Yoko Ichimonji no Kamae* – Open Side Stance
3. *Tenchijin no Kamae* – Heaven Earth & Man Stance
4. *Tenchi no Kamae* – Heaven and Earth Stance
5. *Gedan no Kamae* – Lower Stance
6. *Chudan no Kamae* – Middle Stance

Part Two
Kihon Gata – Basic Techniques

1. *Ukemi* – Blocking
2. *Men Uchi* – Striking the Face
3. *Kote Uchi* – Striking the Wrists
4. *Doh Uchi* – Striking the Torso
5. *Sune Barai* – Sweeping Strike to the Shin
6. *Yoko Men Uchi* – Striking the Side of the Face
7. *Tsuki* – Straight Thrust
8. *Hane Age* – Rising Strike From Below

目 次

Part Three
Kuji no Kata – Nine Seals Techniques

1. *Dai Ippo* – Method One
2. *Dai Niho* – Method Two
3. *Dai Sanpo* – Method Three
4. *Dai Yonho* – Method Four
5. *Dai Roppo* – Method Five
6. *Dai Nanaho* – Method Six
7. *Dai Happo* – Method Seven
8. *Dai Kyuho* – Method Eight

第一章　九鬼神流棒術の起源

延元元年足利尊氏　後醍醐天皇を花山院故宮に幽閉し奉りし時熊野別當藥師丸藏人は其の大逆無道を憤り熊野各庄に飛檄し以て同志を率ゐ潜かに、天皇を御庇護し奉らんとす。

一方藥師丸藏人は實母の里方なる朝臣日野大納言によりて執奏を乞ひたるに　天皇之れを嘉納せらる、卽ち藏人は女裝して　天皇を迎え救ひ奉り將に吉野に至らんとするや逆賊等鬼虎の勢を以て追撃し來り藏人を討ち取らんとす、藏人槍を以て防戰す、槍は二つに折れし

一

Chapter One
The Origins of Kukishin School Bojutsu

In the first year of Engen (1336,) Ashikaga Takauji ordered Emperor Go-Daigo to be confined to the former residence of Emperor Kazanin. Yakushimaru Kurando, who administered Three Kumano Head Shrines, was furious with the traitors to the throne and he immediately sent out a written appeal to every area of Kumano. Having gathered like-minded men, Yakushimaru Kurando secretly led them to protect the Emperor.

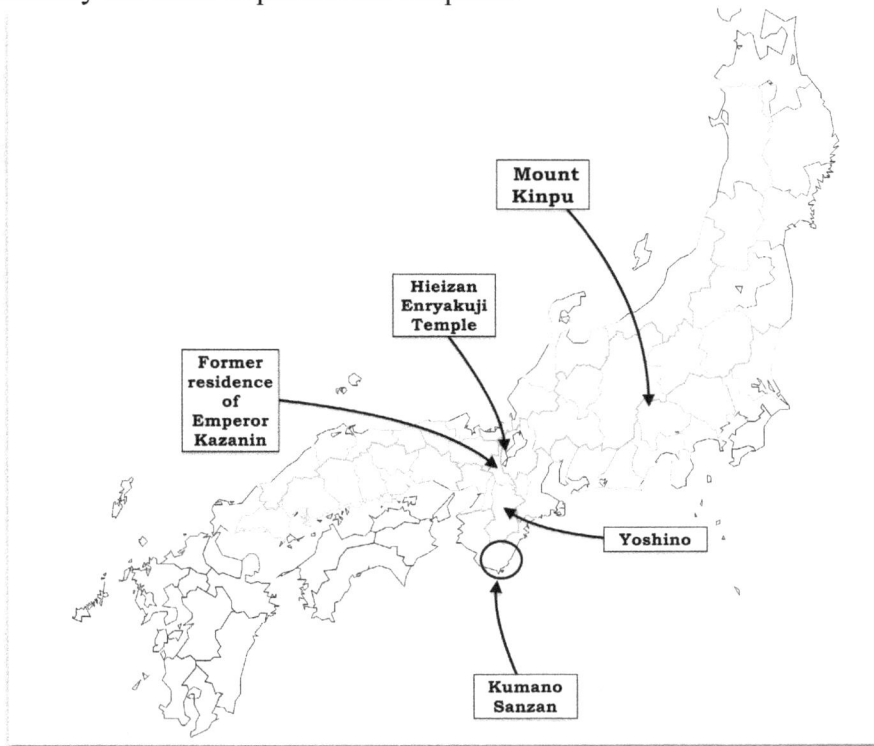

Yakushimaru Kurando asked the Ason-ranked chief councilor of state Hino, who was related to his mother, to inform the Emperor that Kurando would protect him. The Emperor accepted this offer with pleasure. In the end Kurando went to the emperor disguised as a woman and had succeeded in escorting him as far as Yoshino, when they were ambushed by the traitors in a burst of furious violence that would befit a pack of demons.

第一章 九鬼神流棒術の起源

二

られたり、藏人今は必死となり其の折れ槍を六尺棒となして奮戰するに逆賊近寄る能はず、弓矢を以て逆ふ、此時藏人神傳の九字を切るに數千の逆賊共其の神變に打ち驚き忽ち潰亂して退散し、天皇を無事吉野藏王堂に遷幸し奉り假の皇居となす之れ南朝の始めなり。

夫れより藏人は更らに棒術を工夫し九字九通九拾九本を案出す、之れ即ち九鬼神流棒術の起源なり。

The group charged Kurando, trying to kill him, however Kurando defended himself with his Yari, spear. In the course of the fight Kurando's spear was cut in two, however he continued to fight a desperate battle using one end of the broken spear as a Rokushakubo,182 centimeter/ 6 foot wooden staff.

Due to Kurando's fierce resistance the traitors were unable close on their target, so they started shooting arrows at him.

In response, Kurando employed *Shinden Kuji Kiri*, divinely transmitted cutting of the nine seals, and the thousands soldiers that made up the traitor's forces were astonished when they were struck by the divine force the Kuji Kiri released. Thrown into confusion, they retreated in disarray.

Kurando finally succeeded in escorting the Emperor to the temple of the Zao Gongen in Yoshino. The Emperor declared this temple to be the new imperial palace and ushered in the Nancho Era.

Afterwards, Kurando continued to experiment with the Bo, developing new methods. In the end he developed the *Kuji Kutsu Kyujukyu Hon*, Ninety-Nine Techniques that are Infused With the Power of the Nine Seals. This is the origin of the Kukishin School of Bojutsu.

Translator's Note: *Yoshino Zao Gongen*

大勢忿怒の姿を顕して金峯山に
湧現し玉ふ右御手は三鈷を
握り臂を
挙げ左の
手て腸を
押へ二眼明に忿る

Translator's Note: *Yoshino Zao Gongen*

The Yoshino Zao Gongen appears full of wrathful vitality. Zao manifests himself on Mt. Kinpu. In his right hand he holds a three-pronged vajra aloft near his shoulder. His left hand is pushing in his intestines (stomach) His eyes are bright with his dedicated spirit.

From *A Collection of Buddhist Imagery* 仏像図彙 1783
Written by Ito Takemi & Illustrated by Tosa Hidenobu

Zao Gongen is the Shinto manifestation of all three Buddhas: the Historical Buddha, Kannon Bodhisattva and Miroku Buddha, or the Buddhas of the Past, Present, and Future. Buddhist deities transformed into a Shinto deities are called Gongen. Zao Gongen is the protective deity of Mt. Kinpu and Shugendo Practitioners.

Translator's Note: Regarding Kuji

Shinden Kuji-Kiri – The Divinely Transmitted Nine Cuts.

This is a type of ancient magic that originated with Taoist practitioners in China long ago. It began being practiced in Japan after the introduction of Buddhism in the mid-fifth century AD. The Kuji was adopted by practitioners of esoteric Buddhism called Mikkyo. In particular, it is practiced by Shugendo and Yamabushi mountain ascetics who perform intense, ascetic training in the mountains in order to attain enlightenment.

When employing Kuji-kiri, the first two fingers of your right hand represent your sword and you cut a grid of nine lines in the air. (see Overview 1) There are five horizontal and four vertical lines. (see Overview 2)

Each of these lines represents one of nine Kanji and its attributes. (see Overview 3) The lines have to be drawn in the correct order with the correct intent behind each cut. Once completed, the grid serves as a protective barrier, however in the previously described battle with the traitors to the emperor, Kurando employed a method that projected force away from him.

Oftentimes before Kuji-kiri is done, Kuji-in, the Nine Seals, are chanted and specific mudra, hand gestures, are used. In *Kuji Goshin Ho* 九字護身法 *Kuji for Self-Defense* written in 1812, the Buddhist priest known only as Gyochi described Kuji-in as,

A five step process that begins with cleansing the body spiritually and ends with you being protected with a kind of invisible armor, which will deflect evil spirits and allow you to pass through barriers.

Having completed the Nine Seals you will be protected against both physical and supernatural dangers. Gyochi describes this as follows,

This will cause the fresh spirit to descend into your body and calm your mind. This is how you should practice. Kuji can be used when you are travelling over mountains, across vast plains, when travelling alone, when travelling at night or if you are alone in a dark room.

Kuji-Kiri – Cutting the Nine Seals (Overview 1)	
Form the Toh-in, sword seal, with your right and the scabbard with your left.	Insert the sword into the scabbard.
刀 印	
Holding your hands by your left side, draw the Toh-in, sword seal.	Toh-in after drawing it from the sheath at your waist.
 刀 印 を 抜 く 撰	刀 印
Cut the Nine Cuts in the order shown below (Overview 2)	

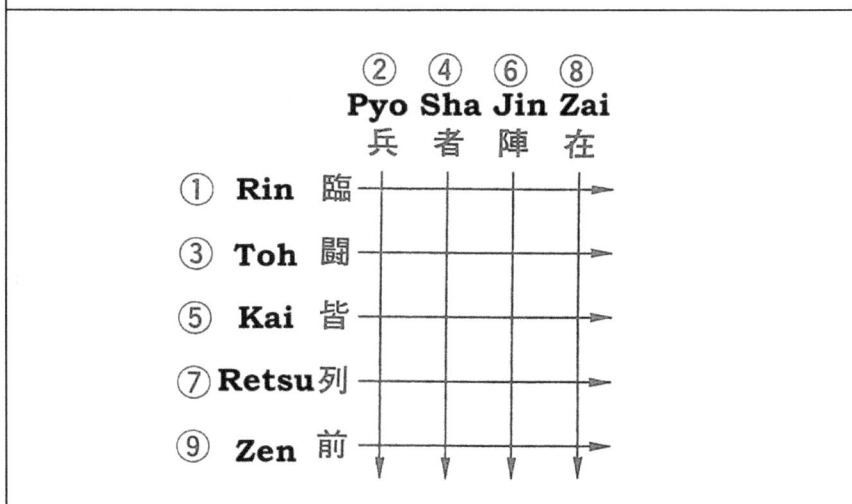

② ④ ⑥ ⑧
Pyo Sha Jin Zai
兵 者 陣 在

① **Rin** 臨
③ **Toh** 闘
⑤ **Kai** 皆
⑦ **Retsu** 列
⑨ **Zen** 前

In addition to the more standard Rin, Pyo, Toh, Sha, Kai, Jin, Retsu, Zai, Zen sequence, the Kukishin School also uses the alternate Kuji sequence, Rin, Pyo, Toh, Sha, Ten, Gen, Shin, Tsu, Riki. The first four Kanji are the same however after Sha, they differ. There is no explanation for how these Kanji are interpreted, however this is their general meaning:

天 Ten - Heaven
元 Gen – Basis
神 Shin – Deity
通 Tsu – Transcend
力 Riki – Power

In addition there is no record of what Mudra are associated with these Kanji. The sequence of lines also differs as shown in the diagram below.

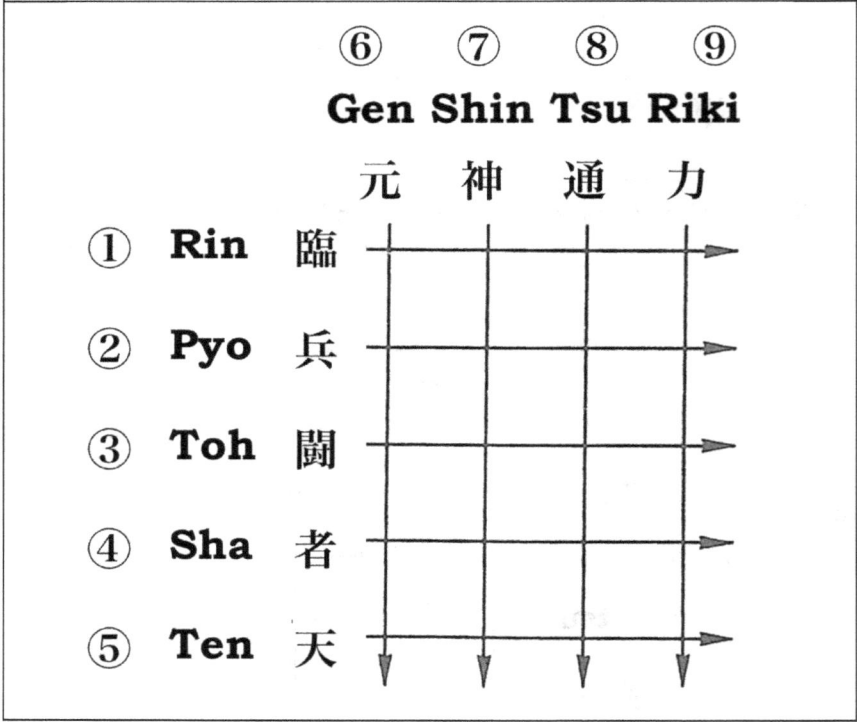

		⑥	⑦	⑧	⑨
		Gen	**Shin**	**Tsu**	**Riki**
		元	神	通	力
① **Rin** 臨					
② **Pyo** 兵					
③ **Toh** 闘					
④ **Sha** 者					
⑤ **Ten** 天					

Kuji-in – The Nine Seals (Overview 3)		
Seal (Mudra)	Kanji	Meaning
	臨 Rin	独鈷印 *Dokko-In* Diamond Thunder Seal
	兵 Pyo	大金剛輪印 *Daikongohrin-In* Golden Wheel of Strength Seal
	闘 Toh	外獅子印 *Gejishi-In* Outer Lion Seal
	者 Sha	内獅子印 *Naijishi-In* Inner Lion Seal
	皆 Kai	外縛印 *Gebaku-In* Outer Binding Seal
	陣 Jin	内縛印 *Naibaku-In* Inner Binding Seal
	烈 Retsu	智拳印 *Chiken-In* Fist of Wisdom Seal
	在 Zai	日輪印 *Nichirin-In* Ring of the Sun Seal
	前 Zen	隠形印 *Ongyo-In* Hidden Shape Seal

第二章 禮儀作法間合

一、道場とは武藝を稽古する所又道義を修業する所を云ふ、道場は最も神聖なる場所で有つて心身を鍛練する所である。

一、道場内に在つては靜肅を守るは勿論常に服裝に注意し、行儀を正し出入の際は神前に禮拜をする。

一、道場には席順が有つて先輩者は後輩者を導き後輩者は先輩者に從順し、同輩者は互ひに謙遜し合ひ、教師の指導をよく守り苟も禮節を亂す等の事が有つてはならぬ。

第二章 禮儀作法間合

三

Chapter Two
Reigi Saho Maai
Manners, Etiquette and Proper Distance

- While a Dojo is a place to train martial arts, it is also a place to train morality. The Dojo is a sacred space for forging the mind and body.

- It goes without saying that when you are in the Dojo you should maintain silence, but you should also always be cautious about what clothes you wear. Maintain proper manners by always offering prayers at the alter when entering and leaving the Dojo.

- The place you sit in the Dojo is prescribed. The Senpai Sha, Senior Members, lead the Kohai Sha, Junior Members and the Junior Members follow the lead of the Senior Members. Dohai Sha, Members of Equal Rank, should exercise modesty and humility when arranging themselves. You should always follow the instructions of your teacher closely and ensure you never falter in your manners in the slightest.

- The position you sit in the Dojo has been established. The Shihan Seki, Instructor Seat, is in the front. To the right, when facing your instructor, is the Joseki, Upper Seat, to the left is the Geseki, Lower Seat.

第二章　禮儀作法間合　　　　四

一、道場には席の定めがあり、普通向つて正面を師範席、師範席に
向つて右を上席、左を下席とする。

一、稽古の始め終りには必ず教師並に先輩者は上席につき、後輩者
は下席につき、神を拝し次で互ひに敬禮をなす。

同輩者なる時は相並んで神を拝し、上席に向つて若くは横に相對
して禮を行ふ。

一、棒術の禮式。

坐禮　右手にて棒の中央を拇指と四指の間に挾みて體の右側に立
てる（第一圖）次で右足を一歩前に踏み出し棒を前に倒すと同時
に左膝を地につける（第二圖）次で棒を引くと同時に右足を退き
右膝を地につけ正坐す、次で兩手を膝の前に突き禮を行ふ。（第三

- At both beginning and the end of every training, the instructors should line up at the front, with the Senior Members arranged starting at the Upper Seat with the Junior Members lined up towards the Lower Seat and offer a prayer to the gods. Then all members should offer their respects to each other.

- If all are Members of Equal Rank, then line up beside each other and offer a prayer to the gods before either turning towards the Upper Seat and bowing or turning to the side and facing each other and bowing.

Bojutsu no Reishiki
How to Bow When Training the Staff

Za Rei
Seated Bow

| One | Two | Three |

Stand holding the Bo on the right side of your body. Hold it in the center between your thumb and other four fingers. This is shown in Picture One.

Next take one step forward with you right foot, dropping down to your left knee, pushing your Bo forward onto the ground at the same time. Next, as shown in Picture Two, pull your right foot and the Bo back at the same time and drop your right knee down so that you end up sitting in Seiza. Finally, as shown in Picture Three, place both hands on the ground in front of your knees and bow.

第二章　禮儀作法間合

第一圖　坐禮ノ一

（ツ圖）

Picture One : Za Rei step one.

第二圖
坐禮ノ二

五

Picture Two : Za Rei step Two.

圖 三 第
坐 禮 ノ 三

第二章　禮儀作法間合

Picture Three : Za Rei step three.

第四圖
立　禮

六

Picture Four : Ritsu Rei.

立禮　は普通練習の場合に行ふ禮で有る。

第四圖の如く棒の中央を拇指と四指の間に挾みて體の右側に立て上體を前に屈めて敬禮を爲す。

それから禮を行ふ時、對手と我れとの間隔卽ち間合は普通六尺である。

一、立合の間合　は相互身體の大小、獲物の長短、等種々の事情に依つて間合を斟酌せねばならぬ。

敵　無手なる場合、我れ三尺棒の時は身構へにより三尺の間合又は五尺の間合が必要である。

敵　太刀、我れ六尺棒なる場合は構へ方により六尺が適當する場合と九尺が適當する場合がある。

Ritsu Rei
Standing Bow

This is the type of a bow typically done during training. As shown in Picture Four, hold the Bo in the center on your right-hand side in between your thumb and four fingers.

When bowing, the Maai, or distance between you and your opponent should be 6 Shaku, 182 centimeters/ 6 feet.

立禮　は普通練習の場合に行ふ禮で有る。第四圖の如く棒の中央を拇指と四指の間に挾みて體の右側に立て上體を前に屈めて敬禮を爲す。それから禮を行ふ時、對手と我れとの間隔卽ち間合は普通六尺である。

一、立合の間合　は相互身體の大小、獲物の長短、等種々の事情に依つて間合を斟酌せねばならぬ。

敵　無手なる場合、我れ三尺棒の時は身構へにより三尺の間合又は五尺の間合が必要である。

敵・太刀、我れ六尺棒なる場合は構へ方により六尺が適當する場合と九尺が適當する場合がある。

第二章　禮儀作法間合

七

Tachi-ai no Maai
Distance for Training

The distance you stand from your opponent when training needs to take into account the relative size of both combatants, the length or shortness of the weapons being employed as well as various other considerations.

When your opponent is Mu-te, or unarmed, then you should stand about 3 Shaku, 90 centimeters/ 3 feet, apart. If you are facing off against an unarmed opponent and you are armed with a Sanjakubo, half-staff, then you should stand 5 Shaku,150 centimeters/ 5 feet, apart.

Generally speaking if your opponent is armed with a Tachi, long sword, and you are armed with a Rokushakubo then a distance of 6 Shaku, 182 centimeters/ 6 feet, is appropriate, however 9 Shaku, 2.7 meters/ 9 feet may be required in some cases.

What this means is that it is necessary to position yourself so that if you take one step forward, you will be able to stab or strike your opponent and if you take one step back you will be able to avoid your opponent's attack.

第三章　姿勢身構　　　　八

故に間合は一歩踏み込めば敵を突き又は撃つ事が出來、一歩退け
ば敵の攻撃を避け得る丈けの間隔を取る事が最も必要な事である。

姿勢

第三章

姿勢身構

正しき姿勢は技術の基礎である。　姿勢が正しければ身體の

Chapter Three
Shisei, Kamae
Posture and Stance

Correct posture is the basis of technique. If your posture is correct then all your movements will be nimble and you will be able to move freely and unobstructed. Since there will be no barrier to your movement, your technique will advance quickly.

諸動作が敏捷自在となり、動作に無理がなく、従つて技術の進歩も速かである。

身體の運動は千變萬化限りなきものであるが故に姿勢は一々之を採れば数限りもないが棒術に於て其中最も多い場合を舉げたならば次の六構へである。

1 平一文字の構へ

2 横一文字の構へ

3 天地人の構へ

4 天地の構へ

5 下段の構へ

6 中段の構へ

第三章 姿勢身構

九

The body is capable of moving in any of a thousand directions before shifting in ten thousand ways, thus if you tried to learn each and every posture, the number would be truly endless. However in Bojutsu the following are the most common postures.

1. *Hira Ichimonji no Kamae* –
   Open Front Stance Like the Kanji for One 一
2. *Yoko Ichimonji no Kamae* –
   Open Side Stance Like the Kanji for One 一
3. *Tenchijin no Kamae* – Heaven, Earth and Man Stance
4. *Tenchi no Kamae*   – Heaven and Earth Stance
5. *Gedan no Kamae*   – Lower Stance
6. *Chudan no Kamae*   – Middle Stance

第三章　姿勢身構

一、平一文字の構

兩手を下げ、棒の三分の一の中を握る。

第五圖
平一文字の構

兩足は少しく左右に開き、顔を正面に向け、自然に安定に直立したる姿勢を云ふ、此の身構は最も變化し易く、又此の姿勢は永く保持することが出來るものである。

（第五圖參照）

一〇

1. *Hira Ichimonji no Kamae*
Open Front Stance Like the Kanji for One 一

Picture Five

Allow your arms to hang down and hold the center third of the Bo. You should stand looking straight ahead with your feet slightly apart. Hira Ichimonji can be described as straight, naturally stable way of standing. This stance is both easy to maintain for a long time as well as the one most adaptable to any situation.

第六圖
横一文字の構

第三章　姿勢身構

二、横一文字の構（左右）

第六圖の如く、體を斜めに顔を正面に向ける。

兩手を下げて棒の三分の一の中を握る。

左足を前に一歩踏み出して膝を少しく曲げて足尖を正面に向ける。

右足は左足の後ろに膝を伸ばして足尖を右向にする。

（第六圖參照）

二一

2. *Yoko Ichimonji no Kamae (Sayu)*
Side Stance Like the Kanji for One 一 (Left and Right)

Picture Six

As Picture Six shows, you are standing looking directly at your opponent who is standing perpendicular to you. Your hands are hanging down holding your Bo in the middle third.

Your left foot should be one step forward with your left knee slightly bent. The toes of your left foot should be pointing towards your opponent.

Your right foot should be behind your left foot with your knee extended and your toes pointing to your right.

三、天地人の構（左右）

第七図の如く、右手は頭上に伸ばし、左手は前に伸ばして棒の三分の一の中を握る、左足を前に一歩踏み出し、膝を少しく曲げ足尖は正面に向ける。

右足は左足の後に足尖を右に向け、膝を伸ばす、又右手を反對に向け握るを逆天地人と云ふ。

第七圖
天地人の構

二二

29

3.*Tenchijin no Kamae (Sayu)*
Heaven, Earth and Man Stance (Left and Right)

Picture Seven

As Picture Seven shows, you are holding the Bo in the center third, with your right hand is raised above your head while your left hand is extended out in front of you.

Take this stance by stepping forward with your left foot, keeping your left knee slightly bent and your toes pointed towards your opponent. Your right foot is behind your left with the toes pointing to your right. Your right knee should be extended. If you switch your right hand around and grip the opposite way, the stance becomes *Gyaku Tenchijin*, Reverse Heaven, Earth and Man Stance.

四、天地の構（左右）

第八圖の如く體を斜めに顔を正面に向ける。棒を右側に引きつけ、右手は肩と略ぼ同じ高さに、左手は水月の高さに於て棒を立てゝ握る。

第八圖
天地の構

第三章 姿勢身構

左足を一歩前に踏み出し膝を少しく曲げ足尖は正面に向ける、右足は左足の後ろに膝を伸し足尖を右に向ける。

一三

4. *Tenchi no Kamae (Sayu)*
Heaven and Earth Stance (Left and Right)

Picture Eight

As Picture Eight shows, you are standing looking directly at your opponent who is standing perpendicular to you. You have pulled your Bo to your right side, and are holding it vertically with your right hand at about shoulder height and your left hand at the same height as Mizuochi, your solar plexus.

Your left foot is one step towards your opponent with your knee slightly bent and your toes pointing at your opponent. Your right foot is behind your left with your toes pointing to your right. Your right knee should be extended.

第三章　姿勢身構

一四

第九圖
下段の構

五、下段の構（左右）

第九圖の如く棒を體の右側にて斜下に向ける。顔を正面に向け、右手は伸ばして右大腿上部の外側に當て、左手は少しく曲げて臍部の邊に置き棒を握る。

左足を一歩前に出し膝を少しく曲げ、足尖を正面に向け、右足は左足の後に膝を伸して足尖を右向け、棒の前端は水月の高さに棒尻は地に附く程度に下げる。

5. *Gedan no Kamae (Sayu)*
Lower Stance (Left and Right)

Picture Nine

As Picture Nine shows, you are holding the Bo angled down on your right side. You are looking directly at your opponent with your right hand extended back holding the Bo against the outside of your right thigh. Your left arm should be bent slightly and grip the Bo at about the height of your navel.

Your left foot should be one step forward with your knee bent slightly and your toes pointing at your opponent. Your right foot is behind your left with your knee extended and your toes pointing to your right. The front end of your Bo should be at about the height of Mizuochi, your solar plexus, while the back end should be low enough so that it is almost on the ground.

六、中段の構（左右）

第十圖の如く左手は伸ばして棒の三分の一の中の前部を握り水月の高さに保ち、右手は棒の三分の一の中の後部を握り臍部の高さに置いて側腹部に密接する、棒尖は敵の目の高さに止め顔を正面に向ける。

左足を前に出し、膝を少しく曲げ足尖は正面に向ける、右足は左足の後に膝を伸ばし足尖を右向きに輕く踏む。

第十圖 中段の構

第三章 姿勢身構

一五

6.*Chudan no Kamae (Sayu)*
Lower Stance (Left and Right)

Picture Ten

As Picture Ten shows, your left hand is extended forward holding a point one third along the Bo, level with Mizuochi, your solar plexus. Your right hand is holding towards the back of the first third of the Bo at about the height of your navel. The Bo should be pressed against your side and the Bo Saki, front end of the staff, should be raised until it is at the height of your opponent's eyes. You should be looking directly at your opponent.

Your left foot is in front with your knee slightly bent and your toes pointing at your opponent. Your right foot is behind your left with your knee extended, your toes pointing to the right and pressing lightly on the ground.

（二）基本形 八本

一、受身、二、面打、三、小手打、四、胴打、五、脛打、六、横面打、七、突キ、八、跳舉の八法あり。

此の形は無理がないから少年は勿論老弱男女の別なく又各人の體質に應じて單獨に誰れにも自由に行ふ事が出來る故に團體々操として又一般家庭に於て之れを朝夕行へば體育上確かに有効且つ其の目的を達せらるゝものと思ふ。

此の棒術基本八法を練習するには目の前に敵が存在するものと假想して練習する事である。

練習するにはイヤー、イョー、エイー等の氣合をかける。

Kihon Gata Happo
Basic Techniques : Eight Methods

1. *Ukemi*   — Blocking
2. *Men Uchi*   — Strike to the Head
3. *Kote Uchi*   — Strike to the Forearms
4. *Doh Uchi*   — Strike to the Torso
5. *Sune Uchi*   — Strike to the Shins
6. *Yoko Men Uchi* — Strike to the Side of the Head
7. *Tsuki*   — Straight Thrust
8. *Hane Age*   — Rising Strike From Below

This method is not particularly difficult so not only will youths be able to learn it, anyone, be they old young man or woman, can train this system. Further, the method can be adjusted to fit any level of physical fitness so that anyone can learn to train this freely. In addition, this training can also be done in groups or by members of a household. I believe that if this training is done every morning and evening, then it will certainly result in improving your health and will help you to achieve your fitness goals.

When training the *Kihon Happo*, Eight Basic Methods, you should imagine that there is an opponent in front of you.

When training you should shout Kiai, shouts unifying body and mind, of *Eyaa! Iyoo!* and *Eii!*

氣合は偉大なる効力を有するものである、我が體力勇氣を奮起すると同時に敵の體力勇氣を喪失せしめて倒すと云ふ意氣込みで力を入れ急激に氣合を懸ける。

又此の棒術を學校生徒や團體等の多數のものに練習さす場合にはイヤー、エイーよりも一、二の懸け聲は動作が敏捷に一致し易い、ラヂオ體操の如くに一二三四五六七八、二二三四五六七八と云ふ風に號令をかける。

練習中は如何なる場合を問わず謹嚴なる態度を以て禮儀作法を行わねばならぬ。

九鬼神流に使用する棒は樫木を直徑八分に丸めたもので其の長さは六尺と四尺二寸、三尺五寸のものである。

第三章　姿勢姿構

一七

Kiai contain a massive amount of power that can be applied to great effect. Not only does it increase your strength and fighting spirit, but it also simultaneously causes your opponent to lose both power and martial vigor, enabling you to topple him. Thus you should pour your energy in your Kiai and release it explosively.

However, when teaching these Bojutsu techniques to classes of students or other large groups, it is better to use commands of *One, Two...* instead of shouts of *Eyaa! Iyoo!* If you do you so it will be easier to unify the movement of everyone in the group and make their technique faster and nimbler. Thus, just like with Radio Calisthenics,[7] you can call out numbers 1,2,3,4,5,6,7,8 and then 1,2,3,4,5,6,7,8 again.

Ensure that whenever you do training you maintain serious and committed attitude while also strictly adhering to manners and proper bowing.

The Bo used in the Kukishin school is a rounded piece of Kashinoki, Oak, and is about 8 Bun, 2.4 cm/ 1 inch, in diameter. It should be 6 Shaku, 182 cm/ 6 feet, 4 Shaku 2 Sun, 127 cm/ 4.2 feet, or 3 Shaku 5 Sun, 106 cm/ 3.5 feet, in length. [8]

---

[7] *Rajio taiso* Radio Calisthenics were introduced to Japan in 1928 to celebrate Emperor Hirohito's ascension to the throne. The exercise program was based on one used Boston starting in 1923.

[8] This book refers to:

The 6 Shaku Bo as Rokushakubo.

The 4.2 Shaku Bo as Jo.

The 3.5 Shaku Bo as Hanbo "Half-Bo."

一、受　身　（左右交代ニ一ヨリ八マデ二回行フ）

一、棒を右手に握りて自然體に立つ。

一、指導者は氣を付けの號令を懸ける。

一、禮の號令により上體を前に屈めて敬禮を行ふ。

一、用意の號令により棒を平一文字に身構へる。（第十一圖）

一、受身の號令。

一、の懸け聲と共に第十二圖の如く左足を一歩前に踏み出すと同時に

左手は前に高く伸ばす。

右手は肘關節を屈曲げて棒を前膊の前側に添はす。

二、の懸け聲と共に左足を元の位置に退くと同時に兩手を下げて平一

1. *Ukemi (Sayu Kotai ni Ichi Yori Hachi Made Ni Kai Okonau)* Blocking (Alternating Both Left and Right, From One to Eight, Repeated Twice)

Picture Twelve
Left Block

Picture Eleven
Hira Ichimonji Kamae

- Hold the Bo in your right hand and stand in *Shizentai*, Natural Stance.
- The *Shidosha*, Instructor, gives the command *Ki wo Tsuke!* Attention!
- At the command of *Rei!* or Bow! bend your upper body forward in a bow of respect.
- At the command of *Yoh-I!* Prepare! shift to *Hira Ichimonji Kamae*. This is shown in Picture Eleven.

The Instructor calls out *Ukemi!* Block! to indicate the technique will begin.

At the command *Ichi!* One! Step forward with your left foot and, at the same time, extend your left arm high above you. The elbow of your right arm should be bent with your right forearm against the shaft of the Bo. This is shown in Picture Twelve.

第十二圖　　　第十一圖

身受左構字文一平

第三章　姿勢身構

文字の構へをな
す。

續いて前の反對
に受身を行ふ。

三の懸聲と共に第
十三圖の如く右
足を前に踏み出
すと同時に右手
は高く前に伸ば
し、左手は肘關
節を屈曲げて棒

一九

43

At the command *Ni!* Two! Return your left foot to its original position and, at the same time, lower both arms so you are in *Hira Ichimonji Kamae* again.

The next step will be practicing blocking on the other side.

Picture Thirteen
Right Block

At the command *San!* Three! step forward with your right foot and, at the same time, extend your right arm high above you. Your left elbow should be bent with your left forearm against the shaft of the Bo. This is shown in Picture Thirteen.

第三章　姿勢　身構

二〇

を前膊の前側に添はす。

の懸け聲と共に右足を元の位置に退くと同時に兩手を下げて平一文字に構へる。

續けて指導者は面打の號令を懸ける。

第十三圖
右受身

二、面打

（左右交代ニ一ヨリ八マデ二回行フ）

一の懸け聲と共に左足を一歩前に

45

At the command *Yon!* Four! Return your right foot to its original position and, at the same time, lower both arms so you are in Hira Ichimonji Kamae.

Next, the instructor will give the command *Men Uchi!* Striking to the Face.

2. *Men Uchi (Sayu Kotai ni Ichi Yori Hachi Made Ni Kai Okonau)* Striking to the Face (Alternating Both Left and Right, From One to Eight, Repeated Twice)

Picture Fourteen
Striking the Face

At the command *Ichi!* One! Step forward with your left foot and, at the same time, use the left end of your Bo to strike your opponent in the face. This is shown in Picture Fourteen.

第十四圖　面を打ちたる所

第三章　姿勢身構

第十五圖　平一文字構

踏み出すと同時に棒の左端を以て敵の面部を打つ。（第十四圖）

二一

Picture Fifteen
Hira Ichimonji Kamae

At the command *Ni!* Two! Return your left foot to its original position and, at the same time, lower both arms so you are in *Hira Ichimonji Kamae*. This is shown in Picture Fifteen.

第三章　姿勢　身搆

二の懸け聲と共に左足を元の位置に退きて平一文字の構へをなす。
（第十五圖）

第十六圖
面を打ちたる所

三

三の懸け聲と共に第十六圖の如く右足を一歩前に踏み出すと同時に棒の右端を以て敵の面部を打つ。

四の懸け聲と共に右足を元の位置に退くと同時に兩手を下げて棒を平一文字に構へる。

面打終らば續いて小手打ち

Picture Sixteen
Striking the Face With *Men Uchi*

At the command *San!* Three! step forward with your right foot and, at the same time, use the right end of your Bo to strike your opponent in the face. This is shown in Picture Sixteen.

At the command *Yon!* Four! pull your right foot back to its original position and, at the same time, lower both arms so you are in Hira Ichimonji Kamae.

After finishing *Men Uchi*, Striking to the Face, the instructor will give the command *Kote Uchi*, Striking to the Wrists.

の號令を懸ける。

三、小手打　（左右交代ニ一ヨリ八マデ二回行フ）

一の懸け聲と共に左足を一歩前に踏み出すと同時に棒の左端を以て
敵の右小手を打ち拂ふ。（第十七圖）

二の懸け聲と共に左足を元の位置に退くと同時に兩手を下て棒を平

一文字に構へる。

三の懸け聲と共に右足を一歩前に踏み出すと同時に棒の右端を以て
敵の左小手を打ち拂ふ。（第十八圖）

四の懸け聲と共に右足を元の位置に退くと同時に兩手を下て棒を平

一文字に構へる。

第三章　姿勢身構

二三

3. *Kote Uchi (Sayu Kotai ni Ichi Yori Hachi Made Ni Kai Okonau)* Striking to the Wrists (Alternating Both Left and Right, From One to Eight, Repeated Twice)

Picture Seventeen
How to Strike the Right Wrist with *Uchi Harau*

At the command *Ichi!* One! step forward with your left foot and, at the same time, use the left end of your Bo to hit your opponent's right wrist with an *Uchi Harau*, Sweeping Strike. This is shown in Picture Seventeen.

At the command *Ni!* Two! return your left foot to its original position and, at the same time, lower both arms so you are in Hira Ichimonji Kamae.

第十七圖
右小手を打ちたる所

第十八圖
左小手を打ちたる所

二四

Picture Eighteen
How to Strike the Left Wrist with *Uchi Harau*

At the command *San!* Three! step forward with your right foot and, at the same time, use the right end of your Bo to hit your opponent's left wrist with an *Uchi Harau*, Sweeping Strike. This is shown in Picture Eighteen.

At the command *Yon!* Four! return your right foot to its original position and, at the same time, lower both arms so you are in *Hira Ichimonji Kamae*.

After finishing *Kote Uchi*, Striking to the Wrists, the instructor will give the command *Doh Uchi*, Striking to the Torso.

小手打ち終らば續いて胴打ちの號令をかける。

四、胴　打　（左右交代ニ一ヨリ八マデ二回行フ）

第十九圖
右胴を打ちたる所

第三章　姿勢身梯

一の懸け聲と共に左足を一歩前に踏み出すと同時に棒の左端を以て敵の右胴を打つ（第十九圖）

二の懸け聲と共に左足を元の位置に退くと同時に兩手を下げて

二五

4. *Doh Uchi (Sayu Kotai ni Ichi Yori Hachi Made Ni Kai Okonau)* Striking to the Torso (Alternating Both Left and Right, From One to Eight, Repeated Twice)

Picture Nineteen
Striking the Right Side of the Torso with *Doh Uchi*

At the command *Ichi!* One! step forward with your left foot and, at the same time, use the left end of your Bo to strike your opponent in the right side. This is shown in Picture Nineteen.

At the command *Ni!* Two! return your left foot to its original position and, at the same time, lower both arms so you are in *Hira Ichimonji Kamae.*

第三章　姿勢身構

第二十圖
左胴を打たち所

二六

棒を平一文字に構へ
る。

三の懸け聲と共に右足
を一歩前に踏み出す
と同時に棒の右端を
以て敵の左胴を打つ

（第二十圖）

四の懸け聲と共に右足
を元の位置に退くと

同時に兩手を下げて棒を平一文字に構へる。

胴打終らば續いて脛打の號令を懸ける。

Picture Twenty
Striking the Left Side of the Torso with *Doh Uchi*

At the command *San!* Three! step forward with your right foot and, at the same time, use the right end of your Bo to strike your opponent's right side. This is shown in Picture Twenty.

At the command *Yon!* Four! return your right foot to its original position and, at the same time, lower both arms so you are in *Hira Ichimonji Kamae.*

After finishing *Doh Uchi*, Striking to the Torso, the instructor will give the command *Sune Uchi*, Striking to the Shin.

五、脛 打（左右交互ニ一ヨリ八マデ二回行フ）

第二十一圖
右脛を打ちたる所

一の懸け聲と共に左足を一歩前に踏み出すと同時に棒の左端を以て敵の右脛を打ち拂ふ。（第二十一圖）

二の懸け聲と共に左足を元の位置に退くと同時に棒を平一文字に構へる。

第三章　姿勢身構

二七

5. *Sune Uchi (Sayu Kotai ni Ichi Yori Hachi Made Ni Kai Okonau)*
Striking to the Shin (Alternating Both Left and Right, From One to Eight, Repeated Twice)

Picture Twenty-One
Striking to the Right Shin with *Uchi Harau*

At the command *Ichi!* One! step forward with your left foot and, at the same time, use the left end of your Bo to strike your opponent in the right shin with an *Uchi Harau*, Sweeping Strike. This is shown in Picture Twenty-One.

At the command *Ni!* Two! return your left foot to its original position and, at the same time, lower both arms so you are in *Hira Ichimonji Kamae.*

第三章　姿勢身構

第二十二圖
左脛を打ち拂ひたる所

三の懸け聲と共に右足を一歩前に踏み出すと同時に棒の右端を以て敵の左脛を打ち拂ふ。（第二十二圖）

四の懸け聲と共に右足を元の位置に退くと同時に棒を平一文字に構へる。

脛打ち終らば續いて横打ちの號令をかける。

二六

Picture Twenty-Two
Striking to the Left Shin with *Uchi Harau*

At the command *San!* Three! step forward with your right foot and, at the same time, use the right end of your Bo to strike your opponent's right shin. with an *Uchi Harau*, Sweeping Strike This is shown in Picture Twenty-Two.

At the command *Yon!* Four! return your right foot to its original position and, at the same time, lower both arms so you are in *Hira Ichimonji Kamae.*

After finishing *Sune Uchi*, Striking to the Shin, the instructor will give the command *Yoko Uchi*, Side Strike.

六、横面打 （左右交代ニ一ヨリ八マデ二回行フ）

第二十三圖
右横面打ち

第三章　姿勢身棒

一の懸け聲と共に左足を一歩前に踏み出すと同時に右手は放し棒の右端を以て敵の右横面を打つ。（第二十三圖）此際左手を添へる。

二の懸け聲と共に左足を元の位置に退くと同時に右手を放し、左手を以て棒を

二九

63

6. *Yoko Men Uchi (Sayu Kotai ni Ichi Yori Hachi Made Ni Kai Okonau)*
Side Face Strike (Alternating Both Left and Right, From One to Eight, Repeated Twice)

Picture Twenty-Three
Striking to the Right Side of the Face

At the command *Ichi!* One! step forward with your left foot and, at the same time, release the Bo with your right hand and swing the right end of your Bo. Strike your opponent in the right side of the face. The moment you make contact your right hand should join your left on the Bo. This is shown in Picture Twenty-Three.

At the command *Ni!* Two! return your left foot to its original position and, at the same time, release the Bo with your right hand. Rotate the Bo around in your left hand, then grab it with your right hand and return to *Hira Ichimonji Kamae.*

64

第三章 姿勢身構

第四十二圖
左横面打ち

を返して平一文字に構へる、此際右手を添へて握る、

三の懸け聲と共に右足を一歩前に踏み出すと同時に左手は放し棒の左端を以て敵の左横面を打つ、此際右手を添へる。（第二十四圖）

四の懸け聲と共に右足を元の位置に退くと同時に左手を放し、右手を以て棒を返して平一文字に構へる。

Picture Twenty-Four
Striking to the Left Side of the Face

At the command *San!* Three! step forward with your right foot and, at the same time, release the Bo with your left hand and swing the left end of your Bo. Strike your opponent in the left side of the face with the left end of your Bo. Your left hand should join your right on the Bo as you strike. This is shown in Picture Twenty-Four.

At the command *Yon!* Four! return your right foot to its original position and, at the same time, release the Bo with your left hand and rotate the Bo around in your right. After you rotate it around, grab it with your left hand and return to *Hira Ichimonji Kamae.*

After finishing *Yoko Uchi*, Side Strike, the instructor will give the command *Tsuki*, Straight Thrust.

横面打終らば續けて突きの號令をかける。

七、突（左右交代ニ一ヨリ八マデ二回行フ）

一の懸け聲と共に左足を一歩前に踏み出すと同時に棒の左端を以て敵の水月部を突く。（第二十五圖）

二の懸け聲と共に左足を元の位置に退くと同時に棒を平一文字に構へる。

三の懸け聲と共に右足を一歩前に踏み出すと同時に棒の右端を以て敵の水月部を突く。（第二十六圖）

四の懸け聲と共に右足を元の位置に退くと同時に棒を平一文字に構へる。

突きが終らば續けて跳舉の號令を懸ける。

第三章 姿勢 身構

三一

7. *Tsuki (Sayu Kotai ni Ichi Yori Hachi Made Ni Kai Okonau)* Straight Thrust (Alternating Both Left and Right, From One to Eight, Repeated Twice)

Picture Twenty-Five
Stepping Forward with the Left Foot and Striking to the Solar Plexus With a Straight Thrust

At the command *Ichi!* One! step forward with your left foot and, at the same time, thrust the left end of your Bo into your opponent's *Mizuochi*, the solar plexus. This is shown in Picture Twenty-Five.

At the command *Ni!* Two! return your left foot to its original position and, lower your hands so that you return to *Hira Ichimonji Kamae.*

Translator's Note: Mizuochi/ Suigetsu – The Solar Plexus

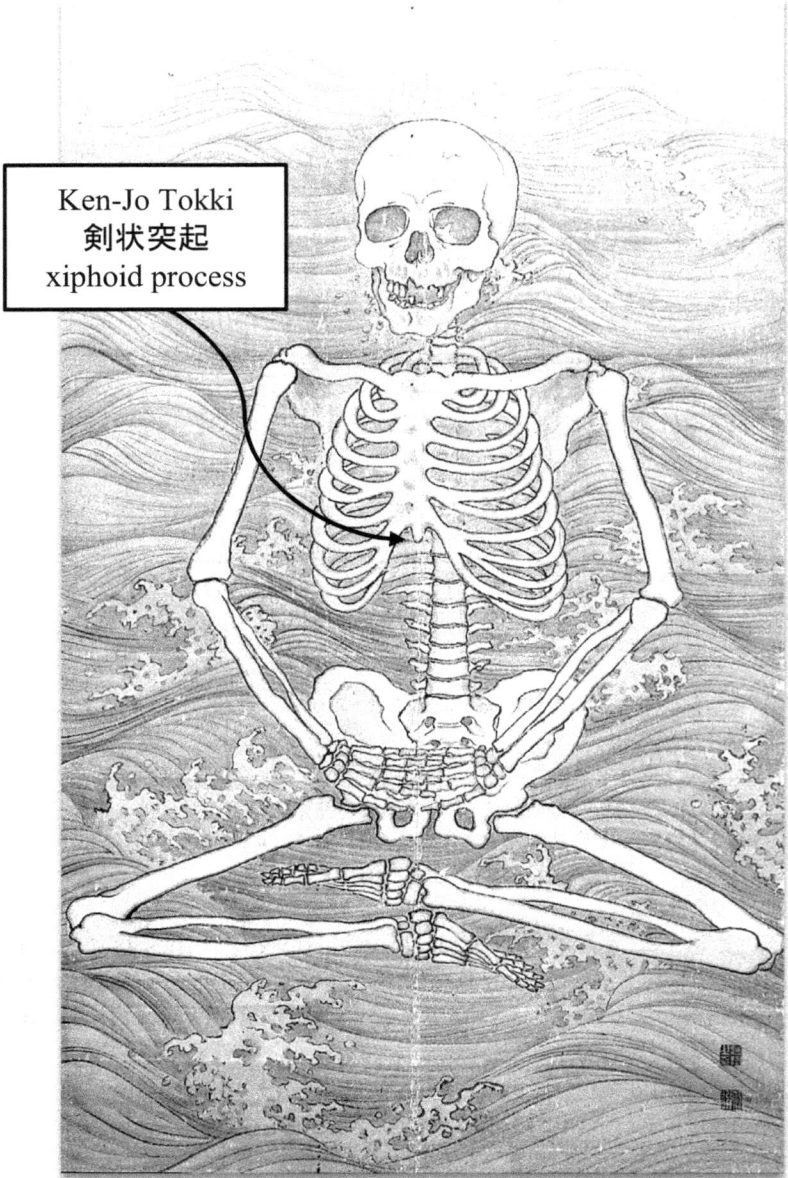

Skeleton Performing Zazen On Waves 波上白骨座禅図
by Maruyama Okyo 圓山應擧 (1733~ 1795)

Translator's Note: Mizuochi/ Suigetsu – The Solar Plexus

While the first Kanji in *Mizuochi* 鳩尾 "pigeon tail" (also read as Mizo-ochi) is Hato 鳩 meaning pigeon, it actually refers to Kakko 郭公鳥 the common cuckoo bird. The bony protrusion at the bottom of the sternum is said to resemble the tail of this bird.

This is called the Ken-jo Tokki, "Sword-shaped protrusion" in contemporary Japanese or the xiphoid process in English. In this book, the two-Kanji combination Suigetsu 水月 "moon reflected on water" is used with the reading *Mizuochi*. *Suigetsu* is another common term for the solar plexus in martial arts books and it is not uncommon to mix the reading and Kanji like this.

第五十二圖
左足を出し水月を突きたる所

第三章　姿勢身構

第六十二圖
右足を出し水月を突きたる所

三二

Picture Twenty-Six
Stepping Forward with the Right Foot and Striking to the
Solar Plexus With a Straight Thrust

At the command *San!* Three! step forward with your right foot and, at the same time, thrust the right end of your Bo into your opponent's *Mizuochi*, the solar plexus. This is shown in Picture Twenty-Six.

At the command *Yon!* Four! return your right foot to its original position and, lower your hands so that you return to *Hira Ichimonji Kamae.*

After finishing *Tsuki*, Straight Thrust, the instructor will give the command *Hane Age*, Rising Strike from Below.

八、跳　擧　（左右交代ニ一ヨリ八マデ二回行フ）

一の懸け聲と共に左足を一歩前に踏み出すと同時に棒の左端を敵の股間に差し入れ睾丸を跳ね擧げる。（第二十七圖）

二の懸け聲と共に左足を元の位置に退くと同時に棒を引いて平一文字に構へる。

三の懸け聲と共に右足を一歩前に踏み出すと同時に棒の右端を敵の股間に差し入れ睾丸を跳ね擧げる。（第二十八圖）

四の懸け聲と共に右足を元の位置に退くと同時に棒を引ひて平一文字に構へる。

八法形終りの號令を懸ける、禮の號令にて敬禮をなす。

第三章　姿勢身構

三三

8. *Hane Age (Sayu Kotai ni Ichi Yori Hachi Made Ni Kai Okonau)* Rising Strike From Below (Alternating Both Left and Right, From One to Eight, Repeated Twice)

Picture Twenty-Seven
Striking Upward to the Groin

At the command *Ichi!* One! step forward with your left foot and, at the same time, thrust the left end of your Bo in between your opponent's legs and strike upward to *Kogan,* the groin. This is shown in Picture Twenty-Seven.

At the command *Ni!* Two! return your left foot to its original position and pull your hands back so that you return to *Hira Ichimonji Kamae.*

第三章　姿勢　身構

第二十七圖

皐丸を跳舉たる所

第二十八圖

皐丸を跳舉たる所

三四

Picture Twenty-Eight
Striking Upward to the Groin

At the command *San!* Three! step forward with your right foot and, at the same time, thrust the right end of your Bo in between your opponent's legs and strike upward to *Kogan*, the groin. This is shown in Picture Twenty-Eight.

At the command *Yon!* Four! return your right foot to its original position and pull your hands back so that you return to *Hira Ichimonji Kamae.*

The next command will be *Happo Gata Owari!* This Ends the Eight Ways of Striking Sequence, followed by *Rei!* Bow! and the sequence will end with mutual bows of respect.

（三）九字の形　九本

第一法

一、棒を右手に握りて自然體に立つ。

一、指導者は氣を附けの號令を懸ける。

一、禮の號令により上體を前に屈めて敬禮をなす。

一、用意の號令により棒を天地人第二十九圖の如くに身構へを爲す。

一、九字の形第一法より第九法まで始めの號令をかける。

第三章　姿勢身構

三五

77

Kuji no Kata Kyu Hon
Nine Seals Techniques Nine Techniques

Dai Ippo
First Method

- Hold the Bo in your right hand and stand in *Shizentai*, Natural Stance.
- The instructor will call out *Ki wo Tsuke!* Attention!
- When the instructor calls out *Rei!* Bow! bend your upper body forward in a bow of respect.
- At the command of *Yoh-I!* Prepare! go into *Tenchijin Kamae* as shown in Picture Twenty-Nine.
- Next the instructor will call out each technique in the Kuji no Kata from Method One through Method Nine.

第二十九圖

天　地　人　の　構

矢　は　次　の　働　作　を　示　す

第三章　姿勢身構

三六

Picture Twenty-Nine
Tenchijin no Kamae
The Arrows Show the Direction of Movement

（第三十圖）（第一法ノ一）

第三章　姿勢身構

敵の左肩を輕く打ちたる所

一の懸け聲と共に右足を一
歩前に踏み出すと同時に
第三十圖の如く敵の左肩
を輕く打つ様にする。

二の懸け聲と共に左足を一
歩前に踏み出すと同時に
敵の右脛を打つ。（第三十
一圖）

三の懸け聲と共に足は其儘
となし第三十二圖の如く
面を輕く打つ様にする。

三七

Picture Thirty
Striking the Opponent's Left Shoulder Lightly

At the command *Ichi!* One! step forward with your right foot and, at the same time, strike as if you are going to hit your opponent lightly on the left shoulder. This is shown in Illustration Thirty.

（二ノ法一節）　圖一十三第

右脛を打ちたる所

第三章　姿勢　身構

三八

四の懸け聲と共に第三十三

圖の如くに棒の尖端を股

間に差し入れて睪丸を跳

ね舉げる。

次で右足より先きに後ろ

に退りつゝ天地人の身構

へをする、此際左足は右

足に遲れぬ様について退

く。

第一法が終らば第二法に

移る。

83

Picture Thirty-One
Striking the Right Shin

At the command *Ni!* Two! step forward with your left foot, striking your opponent in the right shin at the same time. This is shown in Illustration Thirty-One.

第三十二圖（第一法ノ三）
面を輕く打ちたる所

第三章　姿勢身構

（第一法ノ四）第三十三圖

睾丸を跳ね揚げたる所

三九

Picture Thirty-Two
Striking the Face Lightly

At the command *San!* Three! Keep your feet in the same position while striking lightly to your opponent's face. This is shown in Illustration Thirty-Two.

Picture Thirty-Three
Striking Upward into the Groin

At the command *Yon*! Four! Thrust the end of your Bo between your opponent's thighs and strike upward to *Kogan*, the groin. This shown in Picture Thirty-Three.

Tenchijin Kamae

Next, drop back with your right foot and take *Tenchijin Kamae*. Make sure you also pull your left foot back when stepping with your right.

After Method One is finished, next move on to Method Two.

第三章　姿　勢　身　構

第三十四圖　（第二法ノ一）
輕く面を打ちたる所

（第二法ノ二）　第三十五圖

棒を體の右側に引き寄せたる所

四〇

Dai Niho
Method Two

Picture Thirty-Four
Lightly Striking the Face

At the command *Ichi!* One! step forward with your right foot and, at the same time, strike your opponent lightly in the face. This is shown in Picture Thirty-Four.

第二法

一の懸け声と共に右足を一歩前に踏み出すと同時に敵の面を軽く打つ。

二の懸け声と共に右足を一歩前に踏み出すと同時に敵の面を軽く打つ。（第三十四図）

三の懸け声と共に棒尻を以て敵の右胴を拂ひて第三十五図の如くに棒を我が體の右側に引きつけると同時に右足を大きく左足の後に退く。

三の懸け声と共に右足を一歩前に踏み出すと同時に棒尻を以て敵の右脛を打つ。（第三十六図）

四の懸け声と共に棒尖を以て敵の面に向つて打つ様にして右足を後方に退いて天地人の身構へをなす。

第三章　姿勢身構

四一

Picture Thirty-Five
The Bo Pulled Back and Against Your Right Side

At the command *Ni!* Two! use the *Bojiri*, back end of your Bo, to swing with a *Harai*, sweeping motion, towards the right side of your opponent's torso. As you do this, take a big step back with your right foot and plant it behind your left foot while at the same time pulling the Bo back by your right side. Your position after doing this is shown in Picture Thirty-Five.

第三章　姿勢身構

第三十六圖（第二法ノ三）
敵の左脛を打ちたる所

第三十七圖（第二法ノ四）
敵の右脛を打ちたる所

四二

Picture Thirty-Six
Striking Your Opponent's Left Shin

At the command *San!* Three! take a step forward with your right foot and, at the same time, strike with the *Bojiri*, back end of your Bo, to our opponent's left shin. This is shown in Picture Thirty-Six.[9]

At the command *Yon!* Four! withdraw by stepping back with your right foot while bringing the *Bosaki*, front end of your Bo, up as if you are going to strike your opponent in the face. Then take *Tenchijin Kamae.*

After finishing Method Two, move on to Method Three.

---

[9] The text indicates that this is a strike to the right shin, however the picture indicates it is to the left.

第八十三圖
（第三法ノ二）

棒を脊に廻して
敵の面を打たんとする途中

第二法終らば第三法に移る。

第三法

一の懸け聲と共に右足を一歩前に踏み出すと同時に敵の面部を第三十四圖の如く輕く打つ。

二の懸け聲と共に左足を一歩前に踏み出すと同時に敵の右脛を打つ（三十七圖）

四三

95

Dai Sanpo
Method Three

Picture Thirty-Four
Lightly Striking the Face

At the command *Ichi!* One! step forward with your right foot and, at the same time, strike as if you are going to hit your opponent lightly in the face. This is shown in Picture Thirty-Four.

Picture Thirty-Seven
Striking Your Opponent's Right Shin

At the command *Ni!* Two! step forward with your left foot and strike your opponent in the right shin at the same time. This is shown in Picture Thirty-Seven.

Picture Thirty-Eight
After revolving the Bo around your back you are now readying to strike your opponent in the face.

At the command *San!* Three! swing the *Bojiri*, back end of your Bo, to strike your opponent in the face. At the same time, take a big step back with your left foot and spin the Bo so it goes under your left armpit and up behind your back. The correct position is shown in Picture Thirty-Eight.

第三章　姿　姿　身　椬

第三十九圖　（第三法ノ三）
棒を左側に引きたる所

四四

第四十圖　（第三法ノ四）
左足を出し睪丸を跳ね舉げたる所

99

Picture Thirty-Nine
You have pulled the Bo Back By Your Left Side

Use your right hand to swing the Bo into your opponent's face then immediately pull the Bo back by your left side. This is shown in Picture Thirty-Nine.

第四十一圖（第四法ノ一）

天地人の棒

第三章　勢姿身棒

三の懸け聲と共に棒尻を敵の面部に向けて打ち附けると同時に左足を大きく後方に退き棒を左脇より背部に廻し、第三十八圖の如くなし右手に棒を取りて敵の面部を打ち直ちに棒を體の左側に引く。（第三十九圖）

四の懸け聲と共に左足を一歩前に踏み出すと同時に

四五

101

Picture Thirty-Nine
Step Forward With Your Left Foot and Strike the Groin With
a Rising Strike From Below

At the command *Yon!* Four! step forward with your left foot and, at the same time, thrust the *Bojiri*, the back end of your Bo, in between your opponent's legs and strike upward into *Kogan*, the groin. This is shown in Picture Forty. Then immediately drop back and take *Tenchijin Kamae.*

After finishing Method Three, proceed to Method Four.

Picture Forty-One
Tenchijin Kamae

Dai Yonho
Method Four

Picture Forty-Two
Pulling Your Bo Back After Thrusting at Your Opponent's
Solar Plexus

At the command *Ichi!* One! feint like you are going to attack with a straight thrust to your opponent's solar plexus, then immediately pull your Bo back. This is shown in Picture Forty-Two.

第三章　勢姿身構

第四十二圖　（第四法ノ二）
水月を突き棒を引きたる所

四六

第四十三圖　（第四法ノ三）
棒尻を面に打ち附け左掌にて
棒を受け止めたる所

Picture Forty-Three
After striking your opponent in the face with the opposite end
of your Bo, stop the Bo with the palm of your left hand.

At the command *Ni!* Two! throw the *Bojiri*, opposite end of the
Bo, toward your opponent and strike him in the face. You should
catch the Bo with your left hand as shown in Picture Forty-Three.

棒尻を敵の股間に差し入
れ睾丸を跳ね擧げ（第四
十圖）直ちに後方に退り
つゝ天地人に構へる。
第三法終らば第四法に移る。

第四法

一の懸け齊と共に敵の水月
を輕く突きまねをなし直
ちに棒をたぐる（四十二圖）

第三章　姿勢身構

棒を右手にて引きたる所

四七

Picture Forty-Four
Using your right hand to pull the Bo back.

Next, as shown in Picture Forty-Four, immediately pull the Bo back.

（第四法ノ五）　第五十四圖

第三章　姿勢　身棒

皐丸を跳ね擧げたる所

四八

二の懸け聲と共に棒尻を返して敵の面部に打ち附ける此際第四十三圖の如く左手掌にて棒を受け第四十四の如く直に棒を引く

三の懸け聲と共に棒尻を返して敵の股間に差し入れ第四十五圖の如く皐丸を跳ね擧げる。

次で棒を返して面を打つ樣になし天地人に構へる。

Picture Forty-Five
Striking Upwards to the Groin

At the command *San!* Three! throw the *Bojiri*, back end of your Bo, over and thrust the end in between your opponent's legs. Then attack with *Hane Age*, a rising strike, to *Kogan*, the groin, as shown in Picture Forty-Five. Next, flip the Bo over as if you are trying to strike your opponent in the face and instead go into *Tenchijin Kamae*.

After finishing Method Four, proceed to Method Five.

第四十六圖　（五法ノ一）
面を輕く打ちたる所

第四十七圖　（第五法ノ二）
敵の右脛を打ちたる所

第三章　姿勢身構

四九

Dai Goho
Method Five

Picture Forty-Six
Striking Lightly Towards the Face

At the command *Ichi!* One! take a step forward with your right foot and feint as if you are going to strike your opponent in the face. This is shown in Picture Forty-Six.

Then immediately release the Bo with your right hand and rotate the Bo counterclockwise with your left before again grabbing the Bo again with your right hand.

（第四十八圖）　（第五法ノ三）

敵の左脛を打ちたる所

第三章　姿勢身梅

第四法終らば第五法に移る。

五〇

第五法

一の懸け声と共に右足を一歩前に踏み出すと同時に敵の面を打つまねをなし（第四十六圖）直ちに右手を放し、左手を以て逆に棒を一回まわし右手を添へる。

二の懸け声と共に左手を放

113

Picture Forty-Seven
Striking Your Opponent in the Left Shin

At the command *Ni!* Two! release the Bo with your left hand and rotate the Bo around with your right hand one rotation while stepping forward with your left foot. While you are doing this, grab the Bo with your left hand again and strike your opponent in the right shin. This is shown in Picture Forty-Seven.

第四十九圖　（第五法ノ四）

棒を返して一廻し逆天地人に棒へんとする途中

第三章　姿勢身構

し右手を以て一回まわし

つゝ左足を一歩前に踏み

出す途中左手を添へ敵の

右脛を打つ。（第四十七圖）

三の懸け聲と共に右足を一

歩前に踏み出し敵の左脛

を打つ。（第四十八圖）

四の懸け聲と共に棒を返し

て一廻すると同時に右足

を一歩後方に退き同時に

逆天地人に構へる。

五一

Picture Forty-Eight
Striking Your Opponent in the Left Shin

At the command *San!* Three! step forward with your right foot and strike your opponent in the left shin as shown in Picture Forty-Eight.

Picture Forty-Nine
Flipping your Bo over and rotating it one revolution before
taking *Gyaku* (Reverse) *Tenchijin Kamae*

At the command *Yon!* Four! flip the Bo over then spin it once as
you step back with your right foot and take *Gyaku Tenchijin Kamae*.
After finishing Method Five, proceed to Method Six.

Illustration Fifty : *Gyaku Tenchijin no Migamae*

第三章　姿勢　身構

第五十圖　（第六法ノ一）
逆天地人の身構

五二

第五法終らば第六法に移る。

第六法

第五十圖の如く逆天地人の
構へより
一の懸け聲と共に右足を一
歩前に踏み出すと同時に
左手を放し棒を敵の面部
に向つて一回まわして面
を打つ。
二の懸け聲と共に棒尖を右

Dai Roppo
Method Six

Illustration Fifty : *Gyaku Tenchijin no Migamae*
Reverse Heaven, Earth and Man Stance

This technique begins from *Gyaku Tenchijin*, Reverse Heaven, Earth and Man Stance, as shown in Illustration Fifty.

At the command *Ichi!* One! take a step forward with your right foot releasing your grip with your left hand, rotate the Bo around one turn and strike your opponent in the face.

方より左へ頭上にて圓形
に一廻し右胴を打つ。（第
五十一圖）

三の懸け聲と共に棒を左方
より右方に廻して敵の左
胴を打つ。（第五十二圖）

四の懸け聲と共に左手を放
し右手を以て一回まわす
其途中左手を添へ右足を
後方に退くと同時に左手
を放して棒の下方を持ち

第三章　姿勢身構

右胴を打ちたる所

第五十一圖　（第六法ノ二）

五三

Illustration Fifty-One
Striking the Right Side of the Torso

At the command *Ni!* Two! rotate the Bo over your head counterclockwise and strike your opponent in *Migi Doh*, the right side of the torso. This is shown in Picture Fifty-One.

第三章　姿勢　身構

第五十二圖　（第六法ノ三）

左胴を打ちたる所

天地人に構へる。

第六法終らば第七法に移る。

五四

第七法

一の懸け聲と共に右足を一歩前に踏み出すと同時に敵の面部を輕く打つ。（第五十三圖）直ちに棒尻を敵の面部に打ち附け右足を一歩後方に退きつゝ棒

Illustration Fifty-Two
Striking the Left Side of the Torso

At the command *San!* Three! rotate the Bo around clockwise and strike your opponent in *Hidari Doh*, the left side of the torso, as shown in Picture Fifty-Two.

At the command *Yon!* Four! release the Bo with your left hand and use our right hand to rotate the Bo around once. As you are rotating, step back with your right foot and grab the Bo again with your left hand. Then immediately switch your grip with your left hand so you are holding the Bo from below and take *Tenchijin Kamae.*

After finishing Method Six, proceed to Method Seven.

（一ノ法七第）　圖三十五第

面を輕く打ちたる所

第三章　姿勢身構

（二ノ法七第）　圖四十五第

棒を引きたる所

五五

Dai Nanaho
Method Seven

Illustration Fifty-Three
Striking Your Opponent Lightly in the Face

At the command *Ichi!* One! take a step forward with your right foot and lightly strike your opponent in the face. This is shown in illustration Fifty-Three. Then immediately strike your opponent in the face with the *Bojiri,* back end of your Bo.

（第七ノ法三）　第五十五圖

左棒を打ちたる所

第三章　胴　姿　身　勢

五六

を右手の示指と中指の間に挾みて一回まわして面を打つ様にして棒を引く。

（第五十四圖）

二の懸け聲と共に敵の水月を突き直に棒を引く。

三の懸け聲と共に右足を一歩前に踏み出すと同時に敵の左胴を打つ（五十五圖）

四の懸け聲と共に右足を退くと同時に棒を逆天地人

Illustration Fifty-Four
Pulling Your Bo Back

Then step back with your right foot and hold the Bo with just your index and middle fingers. Spin the Bo around and strike your opponent in the face and then pull your Bo backwards.

At the command *Ni!* Two! use a straight thrust to strike your opponent in *Mizuochi*, the solar plexus.

に構へる。

第七法終らば第八法に移る。

第五十六圖（第八法ノ一）
右足を出し棒を左側にて廻す途中

第三章　姿勢身構

第八法

逆天地人の身構へより
一の懸け聲と共に右足を一
歩前に踏み出すと同時に
左手を棒より放し體の左
側に於て右手を以て一廻
し次で第五十六圖の如く

五七

Illustration Fifty-Five
Striking the Left Side of the Torso

At the command *San!* Three! step forward with your right foot and immediately strike your opponent in the left side as shown in Picture Fifty-Five.

At the command Yon! Four! step back with your right foot and take *Tenchijin Kamae.*
After finishing Method Seven, proceed to Method Eight.

第三章　姿勢身姿

第五十七圖　（第八法ノ二）
皐丸を跳ね擧げたる所

五八

左手に棒を握ると同時に
右手は放す。

二の懸聲と共に棒を左手で
半廻し次で右手を添へ右
足を後方に退きつゝ體の
右側に於て棒尻を前に返
して敵の面を打つ様にな
し直ちに棒を手繰る。

三の懸け聲と共に右足を一
歩前に踏み出すと同時に
棒を敵の股間に差し入れ

131

Dai Happo
Method Eight

Illustration Fifty-Six
Your positioning as you step forward with your right foot and are spinning the Bo on your left side.

This technique begins from *Gyaku Tenchijin no Kamae*. At the command *Ichi!* One! step forward with your right foot and, at the same time, release the Bo with your left hand and spin the Bo around before grabbing it again with your left hand. This is shown in Picture Fifty-Six. Then immediately release the Bo with your right hand.

At the command *Ni!* Two! spin the Bo half-way around with your left and grab the Bo with your right hand. Step back with your right foot and flip the *Bojiri*, back end of your Bo, around as if you are trying to strike your opponent in the face, then immediately pull the Bo back.

羂丸を跳ね舉げる。（第五十七圖）

四の懸け聲と共に面を打つ様にして右足を後方に退いて天地人に構へる。

續けて第九法に移る。

第九法

天地人の構へより

一の懸け聲と共に右足を一步

第三章　姿勢身構

第五十八圖　（第九法ノ一）
左肩を輕く打ちたる所

Illustration Fifty-Seven
Striking Upwards to the Groin

At the command *San!* Three! step forward with your right foot and, at the same time thrust the end of your Bo between your opponent's legs and hit with a *Hane Age*, Rising Strike, to Kogan, the groin. This is shown in Picture Fifty-Seven.

At the command *Yon!* Four! strike your opponent in the face and then drop back with your right foot and take *Tenchijin Kamae*.

Next, proceed to Method Nine.

第三章　姿勢　身構

第五十九圖　（第九法ノ一）
右肩を輕く打ちたる所

第六十圖　（第九法ノ三）
面を輕く打ちたる所

六〇

Dai Kyuho
Method Nine

Illustration Fifty-Eight
Lightly Striking the Left Shoulder

This technique begins from *Tenchijin Kamae*.

At the command *Ichi!* One! step forward with your right foot and, at the same time, strike your opponent lightly on the left shoulder. This is shown in Picture Fifty-Eight.

第六十一圖（第九法ノ四）
右手を以て棒を逆に廻し左手を添へたる所

第三章　姿勢身構

前に踏み出すと同時に敵の左肩を輕く打ち（第五十八圖）

二の懸け聲と共に左足を一歩前に踏み出すと同時に棒尻を以て敵の右肩を輕く打つ（第五十九圖）様になし棒を返して第六十圖の如く面を輕く打つ。

三の懸け聲と共に左手は棒を後ろに押し放すと同時

六一

137

Illustration Fifty-Nine
Lightly Striking the Right Shoulder

At the command *Ni!* Two! step forward with your left foot and attack as if you are going to lightly strike your opponent on the right shoulder with the *Bojiri*, the back end of your Bo. This is shown in Picture Fifty-Nine.

Illustration Sixty
Lightly Striking the Face

Then flip the Bo over and, as shown in Picture Sixty, strike your opponent in the face.

Illustration Sixty-One
Your positioning after spinning the Bo counterclockwise with your right hand and then grabbing it with your left hand.

At the command *San!* Three! with your left hand, shove your Bo back and release. At the same time leap back with your right foot while spinning the Bo one revolution counterclockwise and finally grabbing the Bo with your left hand. This is shown in Picture Sixty-One

第三章　姿勢身構

六三

に右足より一歩後方に飛び退りつゝ右手を以て棒を逆に一回まわ

す此の際左手は棒の下方に添へる。（第六十一圖）

四

の懸け聲と共に右足を一歩前に踏み出すと同時に敵の面を打ち棒

尖を右に廻しつゝ右足を後ろに退いて天地人に身構へる。

九字の形終りの號令をかける。

禮の號令にて棒を右足の外側に立て、右足を一歩前に踏み出し棒

を前に倒すと同時に右膝を地に附け次で棒を引くと同時に右足を

退いて右膝を付け正坐し兩手を膝の前に突きて禮をなす。

Tenchijin Kamae

At the command *Yon!* Four! step forward with your right foot and strike your opponent in the face. Then rotate the *Bosaki*, front end of your Bo clockwise while stepping back with your right foot. Finally, take *Tenchijin Kamae*.

The instructor will command, *Kuji no Kata Owari*, This ends the Nine Seals Sequence.

At the command of *Re*i, or Bow, place the Bo on your right side, take one step forward with your right foot and drop down onto your left knee while pushing the Bo flat onto the ground. Next pull the Bo back and, at the same time pull your right leg back and plant your right knee on the ground. Now that you are in *Seiza*, place both hands flat on the ground in front of your knees and bow.

【増補】

（三）九遍の形

此の形は第一法より第九法まで續けて行ふ。

第一法（面、跳）

一、指導者は敬禮の號令をかける、立禮を行ふ。

一、用意の號令にて棒を平一文字に構へる。

一の懸け聲と共に右足を一歩後ろに退きつゝ棒を天地人に構へる。

二の懸け聲と共に右足を一歩前に踏み出すと同時に敵の面を打つ。

三の懸け聲と共に左足を一歩前に踏み出すと同時に棒尻を以つて敵の睾丸を跳ね擧げ

増補

増補

一

Additional Material[10]

(3) *Kyutsu no Kata* – Systematic Overview of All Techniques
This sequence should be done in a continuous flow from steps one to step nine.

Step One
Men, Hane Age
Striking the Face and to the Groin With a Rising Strike

Standing Bow   *Hira Ichimonji no Kamae[11]*

- When the instructor gives the signal to bow, all participants bow from a standing position.
- At the command *Yoh-I*, Prepare, shift your Bo to *Hira Ichimonji Kamae*.

---

[10] This section is titled "Additional Material" and was included at the beginning of the book after the page of corrections. This seems to indicate it was added just before publication. While it is not clear exactly where it this section is supposed to go, following the *Nine Seals Techniques Nine Techniques* seems to be the most logical.

[11] There were no pictures included in this sections, these are included for reference.

Tenchijin no Kamae   ***Men Uchi***

1. At the command of *Ichi*, One, pull your right foot back one step and shift your Bo to *Tenchijin Kamae*.
2. At the command of *Ni*, Two, step forward with your right foot and strike to your opponent's *Men,* face, at the same time.

Hane Age　　　　***Tenchijin Kamae***

3. At the command of *San*, Three, step forward with your left foot and use *Bojiri*, the back end of the Bo, to strike the opponent in the groin with *Hane Age*, rising strike.
4. At the command of *Yon*, Four, draw your left foot back to its original position while shifting your Bo to *Tenchijin Kamae*. (When doing this your left hand should be above your head and your right hand forward.)
5. At the command of *Go*, Five, pull your right foot back and bring both hands down at the same time. Take *Hira Ichimonji Kamae* with the Bo.

增補

二

る。

四の懸け聲と共に左足を元の位置に退きつゝ棒を天地人に構へる。（此際左手は頭上

に右手は前に伸す）

五の懸け聲と共に右足を退くと同時に兩手を下げて棒を平一文字に構へる。

第 二 法 （面、脛）

一の懸け聲と共に右足を一歩後ろに退きつゝ棒を天地人に構へる。

二の懸け聲と共に右足を一歩前に踏み出すと同時に敵の面を打つ。

三の懸け聲と共に左足を一歩前に踏み出すと同時に棒尻を以て敵の右脛を打つ。

四の懸け聲と共に左足を元の位置に退きつゝ棒を天地人に構へる。

五の懸け聲と共に右足を退くと同時に兩手を下げて棒を平一文字に構へる。

Step Two
Men, Sune – Striking the Face and the Shin

Tenchijin Kamae   **Men Uchi**

1. At the command of *Ichi*, One, pull your right foot back one step and shift your Bo to *Tenchijin Kamae*.
2. At the command of *Ni*, Two, step forward with your right foot and strike to your opponent's *Men*, face, at the same time.

Migi Sune   **Tenchijin Kamae**

3. At the command of *San*, Three, step forward with your left foot and use the *Bojiri*, the back end of the Bo, to strike the opponent in *Migi Sune*, the right shin.
4. At the command of Yon, Four, draw your left foot back to its original position while shifting your Bo to *Tenchijin Kamae*.

Hira Ichimonji no Kamae

5. At the command of *Go*, Five, pull your right foot back and bring both hands down at the same time. Take *Hira Ichimonji Kamae* with the Bo.

第 三 法 （面、胴）

一の懸け聲と共に右足を一歩後ろに退きつゝ棒を天地人に構へる。

二の懸け聲と共に右足を一歩前に踏み出すと同時に敵の面を打つ。

三の懸け聲と共に左足を一歩前に踏み出すと同時に棒尻を以て敵の右胴を打つ。

四の懸け聲と共に左足を元の位置に退きつゝ棒を天地人に構へる。

五の懸け聲と共に右足を退くと同時に兩手を下げて棒を平一文字に構へる。

第 四 法 （面、小手）

一の懸け聲と共に右足を一歩後ろに退きつゝ棒を天地人に構へる。

二の懸け聲と共に右足を一歩前に踏み出すと同時に敵の面を打つ。

増補

三

Step Three
Men, Doh – **Striking the Face and the Torso**

Tenchijin Kamae   *Men Uchi*

1. At the command of *Ichi,* One, pull your right foot back one step and shift your Bo to *Tenchijin Kamae.*
2. At the command of *Ni*, Two, step forward with your right foot and strike to your opponent's *Men*, face, at the same time.

Migi Doh Uchi   **Tenchijin Kamae**

3. At the command of *San*, Three, step forward with your left foot and use the *Bojiri*, the back end of the Bo, to strike the opponent in *Migi Doh*, the right side of the torso.
4. At the command of *Yon*, Four, draw your left foot back to its original position while shifting your Bo to *Tenchijin Kamae*.

Hira Ichimonji no Kamae

5. At the command of *Go*, Five, pull your right foot back and bring both hands down at the same time. Take *Hira Ichimonji Kamae* with the Bo.

第三法 （面、胴）

一の懸け声と共に右足を一歩後ろに退きつゝ棒を天地人に構へる。

二の懸け声と共に右足を一歩前に踏み出すと同時に敵の面を打つ。

三の懸け声と共に左足を一歩前に踏み出すと同時に棒尻を以て敵の右胴を打つ。

四の懸け声と共に左足を元の位置に退きつゝ棒を天地人に構へる。

五の懸け声と共に右足を退くと同時に両手を下げて棒を平一文字に構へる。

第四法 （面、小手）

一の懸け声と共に右足を一歩後ろに退きつゝ棒を天地人に構へる。

二の懸け声と共に右足を一歩前に踏み出すと同時に敵の面を打つ。

増補

三

Step Four
Men, Kote – Striking the Face and the Wrists

Tenchijin Kamae   *Men Uchi*

1. At the command of *Ichi*, One, pull your right foot back one step and shift your Bo to *Tenchijin Kamae*.
2. At the command of *Ni*, Two, step forward with your right foot and strike to your opponent's *Men*, face, at the same time.

Migi Kote   **Tenchijin Kamae**

3. At the command of *San*, Three, step forward with your left foot and use the *Bojiri*, the back end of the Bo, to strike the opponent in *Migi Kote*, the right wrist.
4. At the command of *Yon*, Four, draw your left foot back to its original position while shifting your Bo to *Tenchijin Kamae*.

Hira Ichimonji no Kamae

5. At the command of *Go*, Five, pull your right foot back and bring both hands down at the same time. Take *Hira Ichimonji Kamae* with the Bo.

増補

四

三の懸け聲と共に左足を一歩前に踏み出すと同時に棒尻を以て敵の右小手を打つ。

四の懸け聲と共に左足を元の位置に退きつゝ棒を天地人に構へる。

五の懸け聲と共に右足を一歩後ろに退くと同時に兩手を下て棒を平一文字に構へる。

第五法 (面、突)

一の懸け聲と共に右足を一歩後ろに退きつゝ天地人に構へる。

二の懸け聲と共に右足を一歩前に踏み出すと同時に敵の面を打つ。

三の懸け聲と共に左足を一歩前に踏み出すと同時に棒尻を以て敵の水月を突く。

四の懸け聲と共に左足を元の位置に退きつゝ棒を天地人に構へる。

五の懸け聲と共に右足を退くと同時に兩手を下げて棒を平一文字に構へる。

Step Five
Men, Tsuki – Striking the Face and Striking with a Straight Thrust

Tenchijin Kamae   *Men Uchi*

1. At the command of *Ichi,* One, pull your right foot back one step and shift your Bo to *Tenchijin Kamae.*
2. At the command of *Ni,* Two, step forward with your right foot and strike to your opponent's *Men,* face, at the same time.

Tsuki Uchi

Tenchijin Kamae

3. At the command of *San*, Three, step forward with your left foot and use the *Bojiri*, the back end of the Bo, to strike with a *Tsuki*, straight thrust, aimed at *Suigetsu*, the solar plexus.
4. At the command of *Yon*, Four, draw your left foot back to its original position while shifting your Bo to *Tenchijin Kamae*.

Hira Ichimonji no Kamae

5. At the command of *Go*, Five, pull your right foot back and bring both hands down at the same time. Take *Hira Ichimonji Kamae* with the Bo.

第六法（突、胴）

一の懸け聲と共に右足を一歩後ろに退きつゝ棒を天地人に構へる。

二の懸け聲と共に左足を一歩前に踏み出すと同時に右足は左足に遲れぬ様に續いて進み敵の水月を突く。

三の懸け聲と共に右足を一歩右前隅に踏み出すと同時に棒尻を以て敵の左胴を打つ。

四の懸け聲と共に右足を後に大きく退きつゝ棒を天地人に構へる。

五の懸け聲と共に左足を退くと同時に兩手を下げて棒を平一文字に構へる。

第七法（突、脛）

增補

一の懸け聲と共に右足を一歩後に退きつゝ棒を天地人に構へる。

五

Step Six
Tsuki, Doh –Striking With a Straight Thrust and Striking the Torso

Tenchijin Kamae

Tsuki Uchi

1. At the command of *Ichi*, One, pull your right foot back one step and shift your Bo to Tenchijin Kamae.
2. At the command of *Ni,* Two, step forward with your left foot and, at the same time, slide your right foot forward, ensuring you maintain the same distance between your feet. Strike with a *Tsuki*, straight thrust, to *Suigetsu*, your opponent's solar plexus.

Hidari Doh Uchi   **Tenchijin Kamae**

3. At the command of *San*, Three, step diagonally to your right
    with your right foot and strike to your opponent's *Hidari Doh*,
    left side of the torso, with the *Bojiri,* the back end of your Bo.
4. At the command of *Yon*, Four, take a big step back with your
    right foot back while shifting your Bo to *Tenchijin Kamae*.

Hira Ichimonji no Kamae

5. At the command of *Go*, Five, pull your left foot back while bring both hands down at the same time. Take *Hira Ichimonji Kamae* with the Bo.

増補　　　　　　　　　　　　　　　　　　六

二の懸け聲と共に左足より一歩前に踏み出すと同時に右足は左足に遲れぬ様に續いて進み、敵の水月を突く。

三の懸け聲と共に右足を一歩右前隅に踏み出すと同時に棒尻を以て敵の左脛を打ち拂ふ。

四の懸け聲と共に右足を後ろに大きく退きつゝ棒を天地人に構へる。

五の懸け聲と共に左足を退くと同時に兩手を下げて棒を平一文字に構へる。

第 八 法 （突、跳）

一の懸け聲と共に右足を一歩後に退きつゝ棒を天地人に構へる。

二の懸け聲と共に左足より前に一歩踏み出すと同時に右足は左足に遲れぬ様に續いて進み、敵の水月を突く。

167

Step Seven
Tsuki, Sune – Striking With a Straight Thrust and Striking the Shin

Tenchijin Kamae   *Tsuki Uchi*

1. At the command of *Ichi*, One, pull your right foot back one step and shift your Bo to *Tenchijin Kamae*.
2. At the command of *Ni*, Two, step forward with your left foot and, at the same time, slide your right foot forward, ensuring you maintain the same distance between your feet. Strike with a *Tsuki*, straight thrust, to *Suigetsu*, your opponent's solar plexus.

Hidari Sune

Tenchijin Kamae

3. At the command of *San*, Three, step diagonally to your right with your right foot and strike to your opponent's *Hidari Sune*, left shin, with the *Bojiri*, the opposite end of your Bo.
4. At the command of *Yon*, Four, take a big step back with your right foot back while shifting your Bo to *Tenchijin Kamae*.

Hira Ichimonji no Kamae

5. At the command of *Go*, Five, pull your left foot back while bring both hands down at the same time. Take *Hira Ichimonji Kamae* with the Bo.

三の懸け聲と共に右足を一歩前に踏み出すと同時に棒尻を以つて敵の下段を跳ね舉げる。

四の懸け聲と共に右足を後ろに大きく退きつゝ棒を天地人に構へる。

五の懸け聲と共に左足を退くと同時に兩手を下げて棒を平一文字に構へる。

第九法 (突、小手)

一の懸け聲と共に右足を後に一歩退きつゝ棒を天地人に構へる。

二の懸け聲と共に左足より一歩前に踏み出すと同時に右足は左足に遅れぬ様に續いて進み、敵の水月を突く。

三の懸け聲と共に右足を一歩右前隅に踏み出すと同時に棒尻を以て敵の左小手を下より打ち拂ふ。

増補

七

171

Step Eight
Tsuki, Hane Age – Striking With a Straight Thrust and Striking With a Rising Attack From Below

Tenchijin Kamae

Tsuki Uchi

1. At the command of *Ichi,* One, pull your right foot back one step and shift your Bo to *Tenchijin Kamae*.
2. At the command of *Ni*, Two, step forward with your left foot and, at the same time, slide your right foot forward, ensuring you maintain the same distance between your feet. Strike with a *Tsuki*, straight thrust, to *Suigetsu*, your opponent's solar plexus.

Hane Age   ***Tenchijin Kamae***

3. At the command of *San*, Three, step forward with your right
    foot and strike *Gedan*, lower part of your opponent's body (the
    groin,) with a *Hane Age*, rising strike, using the *Bojiri,* the
    back end of your Bo.
4. At the command of *Yon*, Four, take a big step back with your
    right foot back while shifting your Bo to *Tenchijin Kamae*.

Hira Ichimonji no Kamae

5. At the command of *Go*, Five, pull your left foot back while bring both hands down at the same time. Take *Hira Ichimonji Kamae* with the Bo.

Step Nine
Tsuki, Kote – **Striking With a Straight Thrust and Striking the Forearms**

Tenchijin Kamae   ***Tsuki Uchi***

1. At the command of *Ichi*, One, pull your right foot back one step and shift your Bo to Tenchijin Kamae.
2. At the command of *Ni*, Two, step forward with your left foot and, at the same time, slide your right foot forward, ensuring you maintain the same distance between your feet. Strike with a *Tsuki*, straight thrust, to *Suigetsu*, your opponent's solar plexus. [12]

---

[12] The technique ends on this page and steps 4 and 5 were omitted. However it is likely that they followed the same pattern as the previous ones so they have been included.

Hidari Kote Uchi

Tenchijin Kamae

3. At the command of *San*, Three, step diagonally to your right with your right foot and hit with sweeping strike from below to your opponent's *Hidari Kote*, left forearm, with the *Bojiri*, the back end of your Bo.
4. At the command of *Yon*, Four, take a big step back with your right foot back while shifting your Bo to *Tenchijin Kamae*.

Hira Ichimonji no Kamae

5. At the command of Go, Five, pull your left foot back while bring both hands down at the same time. Take *Hira Ichimonji Kamae* with the Bo.

End of Part One

KOBA KOSHIRO・ERIC SHAHAN

Translator's Note: Training Weapons

捕手術練習武器各種販賣

一、十手　　　　　　　　　　金壹圓

二、杖（樫三尺棒）　　　　　金壹圓

三、短刀（代用木刀九寸五分）金參拾錢

四、刀劍（代用樫木劍）　　　金壹圓參拾錢

五、槍又は棒（代用樫六尺棒）金七拾錢

右捕手術練習用武器各種御便宜を計り實費を以て御取次販賣致候但し別に送料は實費申受け候

東京市麴町區飯田町六丁目廿一番地

合名會社　文　武　書　院　代理部

電話九段二七三三番◇振替東京四六三九三番

Translator's Note: Training Weapons

This book give no indication of how much training weapons cost, however the book *Torite Jutsu Kaisetsu* 捕手術解説, A Guide to Police Arresting Techniques, by Horita Sutejiro published in Showa 7 (1932) contains a list of prices

Martial arts weapons catalogue
1932
1. Jutte – 1 Yen [13]
2. Jo (Oak 3 Shaku Bo) – 30 Sen[14]
3. Tanto (training wooden sword 9 Sun, 5 Bun) – 30 Sen
4. Token (Oak training sword) – 1 Yen 30 Sen
5. Yari (spear) or Bo (6 Shaku wooden training pole) – 70 Sen[15]

Shipping and handling separate

---

[13] One Yen in 1932 is equivalent to about $13.70 today.
[14] 1 Sen is 1/100th of a Yen.
[15] The pole can be used either as a staff or as a spear.

www.ingramcontent.com/pod-product-compliance
Lightning Source LLC
Chambersburg PA
CBHW061730270326
41928CB00011B/2176